DISRUPTING
AFRICA

THE RISE AND RISE OF AFRICAN INNOVATION

NNAMDI ORANYE

CONTENTS

TAKING ON SILICON VALLEY:
HOW AFRICA'S INNOVATORS WILL SHAPE ITS FUTURE

FOREWORD

O ut of the new generation of right-thinking African professionals I have been blessed to know in my African business evangelism and media work comes this well-timed gem. Disrupting Africa — The Rise & Rise of African Innovation is precisely what Africa and the world have been waiting for: a celebration of cutting edge innovations that are tectonically shifting the way Africa does business.

This is an easy-to-read anecdotal portrayal of cardinal inventions or innovations that span healthcare, facilitating access to financial services, transport, energy, agriculture, arts and entertainment. These innovations are either by Africans or global citizens — just like Nnamdi, the author — who appreciate that they have an active role to play in improving the quality of life in what will be the world's most attractive investment destination for the next couple of decades.

Check out the stories of MicroEnsure, which has virtually made insurance without premiums possible, to M-Kopa — that pay as you go energy solution — to Sproxil, a simple solution to the deadly scourge of fake medicines. Most of these innovations have been the subject of exhilarating conversation on my radio show, Power Hour on Power FM 98.7, where Nnamdi is a weekly contributor. Nnamdi was introduced to the Power Hour family of freelance analysts and commentators on July 16th in 2015. I had met him only two days before, thanks to Antoinette Prophy — CEO of AfroFusion — who had asked me to consider inviting him as a guest from time to time. She believed that 'he could add value talking about disruptive innovation'. He has been a weekly feature since and I'm not going to let him go anywhere else!

It was not surprising, therefore, that in late 2015 he shared his plans to write a book about innovation. Just as he had thought at our first meeting that we would have a long planning phase before his first appearance, I reckoned he was simply thinking about writing. Was I wrong!

In March 2016 I had his manuscript, and he was itching to publish. I commend Nnamdi for sampling an enduring business passion of his in a format that all can enjoy. This is a must-read reference book for anyone inspired by Africa, the potential it offers, innovation, and for everyone interested in seeing opportunity in every backlog.

Africa has been through a lot at the hands of colonial exploitation, which divided this beautiful continent with the help of corrupt and greedy leaders. The time for young inspired Africans has come. To effect the requisite positive change to the fortunes of Africa, they need to claim their voice. They need to, in the words of Maya Angelou, not be the 'caged bird' that 'stalks down his narrow cage' because its inability to 'see through his bars of rage' will forever mean that his 'wings are clipped and his feet are tied'. To 'claim the sky', Angelou offers an alternative scenario to the caged (African) bird. The free bird, instead, 'leaps on the back of the wind and floats downstream - till the current ends and dips his wing in the orange sun's rays'.

Nnamdi, with this book, is profiling and celebrating those who have done that. They are leaping on the back of the wind called the 'Africa Rising' narrative. They are claiming the sky, from which they are able to show us all the possibilities that lie beyond our bars of rage due to what happened to us in the past and that which continues to enslave us.

Innovation rightly knows no political borders, respects no tradition, and always takes the majority forward. Africa's billion people are hungry for this. They need it as much as they need oxygen. Investors long for it. Equally, Africa and the world need to know about innovation when it happens.

This book — aptly titled Disrupting Africa - gives the reader a glimpse in a relaxed, yet energised, manner.

Enjoy the cruise!

— Victor Kgomoeswana
Award-Winning Presenter And Author

PREFACE

I must confess, I never grew up thinking I'll be passionate about Africa. I never imagined that I'll be passionate about innovation. I never imagined ever writing this book.

But here I am.

I vividly remember sitting in the lounge at the Hyatt, Rosebank in South Africa, with Victor Kgomoeswana and a mutual acquaintance, talking about Africa and how innovation was rapidly changing the way we view the motherland. I could have sworn we were wired on the same frequency that day — Victor, visibly passionate about the continent, me enamoured about innovation in it. I was in this bubble of excitement until he broke it by saying, "I want you on the show this Thursday to talk about innovation. We will start a weekly innovation segment!"

I thought I would have weeks to prepare for my foray into the radio world, but I was to be thrown into the deep end. Not that I minded! My first segment was particularly overwhelming — predominantly because I realised there were quite a number of people out there who shared the same passion I had for innovation in Africa, and how it can change the way we view our continent. After launching quite a number of innovations for large multi-nationals in Africa — a digital payment app for parking, an international remittance product, a digital credit card platform, to name a few, I thought only a few people got excited by the topic. Boy, was I wrong! You should have seen the frantic expressions in the studio with the producers, as the lights lit up with callers! It was a very humbling experience and one that encouraged me to put pen to paper.

Being an avid reader, I'm always on the search for well written business books about Africa. Outside of Victor Kgomoeswana's Africa is Open for Business and more recently, Ashish Thakkar's The Lion Awakens, I've been hard-pressed to find any business book that inspires the African entrepreneur with practical on-the-ground experiences. Don't get me wrong, Western business books do have a place in the continent, but I await the day that our bookstores are flooded with experiences of African entrepreneurs who made it (and those who didn't) so that we can begin to see our Africa in a different light.

I'll present many facts and figures in this book, but these don't do justice to the opportunity that presents itself in our motherland. One of my popular lines on the radio show and speaking at conferences is, "You can't remote control investing in Africa. You have to be in Africa". It's really true. No number of reports, news headlines, books or articles will prepare you for the opportunities (and challenges) that you will experience in being in Africa.

Anyone who has done business in Africa will know this. You can have an absolutely brilliant meeting in Lagos, Nigeria or Nairobi, Kenya; go back to your home country; send your follow-up emails and potentially get no or limited responses. In frustration, you fly back three months later because you were so close to closing the deal. You're welcome back with open arms and you pick up conversations like you never left! At first, I thought this was a weird way to do business, but when reflecting deeper I realised that what Africa is asking of you is: "Are you here to stay?"

I am deliberately not going to focus on the macro-economic opportunities in the continent or talk about the challenges most Africans face in trying to upscale. I highly recommend both

Victor and Ashish's books where they delve deep into their experiences in travelling far and wide across my continent. I catch myself smiling when I read certain chapters of their books as they accurately reflect my own experiences.

What I will do however, is focus on what I'm passionate about: innovation in Africa. Being fortunate enough to have lived on three continents, and five different countries, I've come across different levels of appetite for innovation. What I can categorically state is that Africa is well and truly ahead of the developed world when it comes to innovation. It's not that the developed world doesn't want to be innovative, but the reality is that the systems that worked two decades ago still work today — so there's an undercurrent of "why change it?". In Africa, we literally have a clean canvas to innovate from, due to our lack in what has become traditional infrastructure. We are fortunate to have governments and institutions willing to try new things, and we are further blessed with the worlds youngest population. Put all this in the innovation melting pot and fireworks are definitely sure to explode. As indeed they are!

I've been privileged to present and chair various conferences around Africa and one thing that continuously stands out is the quality of young professionals and entrepreneurs at these conferences. One is tempted to think that they've worked or studied outside of the continent but they are mostly home-grown talent. This makes me believe that we are on the right trajectory. In fact, my mantra to friends and colleagues outside of the continent has been this: Now is the time to come back home.

I was honoured in 2015 to listen to the former President of South Africa, Thabo Mbeki speak at the HomeComing Revolution Conference. Aside from being awestruck that I was literally seated an arm's length from the former President Mbeki,

I was thoroughly blown away by his keynote speech encouraging Africans to come back home. The conference spoke deeply to me (also being a 'returnee' to the continent) and I realised that we, as Africans, have a role to play in changing the African narrative. Imagine the African brain power that's out there, developing technology, outside of Africa. Imagine if they did it for the motherland.

In this book, I humbly attempt to present some disruptive innovation and entrepreneurs changing the narrative. Most of these innovative African businesses I've come across either at conferences, in my professional sojourns, or have been featured on my weekly radio show. In capturing their stories in this book, I'm hoping that the next wave of African entrepreneurs and innovators are inspired to continuously push their boundaries and step into the Africa they want to see in the next decade. There was so much to include, actually, that I literally had to tell myself to stop several times so that I could get this book published! This is a reflection of how quickly innovation is springing up on the continent and how this is maturing and having an impact across Africa.

Innovation is, well, always innovating. It's hard to write a book on innovation that will still be relevant in five years! If I find my book outdated by then, I will smile. Because it's a good thing. It means the African innovation landscape is moving fast and new innovation is being adopted. Every week I prepare for my innovation radio segment I can see new waves of innovation coming through. I'm continuously amazed and excited by the innovation that keeps coming out of the continent. It really is a thoroughly exciting time for us to be in Africa.

The Legend of Africa begins.

INNOVATION NOTE

In the spirit of innovation, this book contains links to relevant videos, various podcasts of the innovation segment on PowerFM 98.7, as well as social media profiles for innovators. The printed version incorporates QR codes which you can scan using any QR scanning app, available through your phone's app store (just search for "QR code"). The e-book version lets you tap the codes and access the links directly. Snippets of the book will be featured on my social media profile and, as with any digital media implementation, links, profiles and videos may get refreshed or broken — but we'll endeavour to keep them as up-to-date as possible.

"I think we need to change the narrative. People are talking about bringing Silicon Valley to Africa. I'm a believer that rather than trying to bring Silicon Valley to Africa, let's bring Africa to Silicon Valley. I think it's time we, as Africa, become innovative; create solutions that we can take global rather than trying to reinvent what has already been done."

- Ashish J. Thakkar, Founder and Md of Mara Group

CHAPTER ONE

AFRICA IS READY FOR LIFT-OFF

I can easily recall my first foray back into Africa after leaving for Australia at the age of 26. I hadn't planned to return so soon — it had only been two years earlier I left for Australia. But I was at the Australian Open with a good friend of mine, Christopher Lane, discussing his business, MTIL at the time. He sold pre-paid scratch cards. Yes, remember them? He had much success printing these cards at his Indian factory and distributing them across the Pacific islands, and he was keen to expand into Africa.

"Why don't you set up my African office in South Africa?" he asked, while I was trying to keep my eyes on the game. Being only 26 at the time, and just having a few years in the professional work force, this was way too left-field for me to even comprehend. But another side of me piped up, asking, "Why not?"

And hence begun my sojourn to the motherland. I ended up travelling far and wide through the continent — Ghana, Nigeria, Kenya, Tanzania, Namibia, Botswana, South Africa and much more. Bright eyed and bushy tailed, I ventured into mobile operators' offices speaking with C-Level executives, punting my wares. What I recall vividly is realising that in 2006 the market was fast moving into an innovative space. This was way before being able to buy airtime from your bank account was mainstream. Innovation was palpable and you could just feel it in the air.

Fast forward ten years later and you can see how far things have come. Not only has Africa leapfrogged the developed world in quite a number of aspects, we've also now started exporting some of our innovation. I can only imagine what the next decade will look like.

Africa is, without a shadow of a doubt, ready for lift off. Marieme Jamme of the BBC once called it the "hottest date in town".[1] I've felt that this has been a clear proclamation for over half a decade, with the 2010 FIFA World Cup in South Africa finally bringing to the public what research companies and those in the know already knew. You might recall the slogan: Ke Nako, Tswana for It's Time. Africa has felt that it has been Time for quite some time, and for good reason too.

After a long time of simmering, things are definitely on the boil. As Victor Kgomoeswana suggests in Africa is Open for Business, "Any company that dreams of sustainable growth and return on investment knows that the greater risk is not being in Africa, but not being in Africa."[2] For just under a decade, research firms and respected journalistic sources have completely changed their tune on the continent. Perhaps one of the most memorable was The Economist's December 2011 piece, The Sun Shines Bright, which was a massive turnaround from its previous pessimistic

---

1   *Reinventing technology in Africa for Africans* (2014). Accessed at www.bbc.com/future/story/20120810-reinventing-technology-in-africa

2   *Africa is Open for Business* by Victor Kgomoeswana. (Pan Macmillan Publishers, EAN: 978-1-77010-372-6, Chapter 2.

views on the continent. Here's a snippet of it:

"Since The Economist regrettably labelled Africa 'the hopeless continent' a decade ago, a profound change has taken hold. Labour productivity has been rising. It is now growing by, on average, 2.7% a year. Trade between Africa and the rest of the world has increased by 200% since 2000. Inflation dropped from 22% in the 1990s to 8% in the past decade. Foreign debts declined by a quarter, budget deficits by two-thirds. In eight of the past ten years, according to the World Bank, sub-Saharan growth has been faster than East Asia's (though that does include Japan)."[3]

It has continued in this vein. "Growth forecasts of around 5% for 2015 are among the highest in the world even though oil continues its plunge and other commodities like copper, cotton and platinum are trading close to 52 week lows," says researcher Kevin O' Marah, citing that the reason for all this is consumer spending. "Today however, an emerging middle class and an increasingly connected population of nearly one billion wants, and is ready, to pay for consumer goods like those sold in Europe and the U.S."[4]

The Harvard Business Review adds, "Africans spend nearly $900 billion on goods and services — far more than Indians do. Pent-up consumer demand on the continent is enormous, and so are the opportunities: Consider that telecom companies have added 316 million subscribers — more than the U.S. population

---

3   See The Economist online, *The Sun Shines Bright*, accessed at www.economist.com/node/21541008

4   As stated at Forbes Magazine, *Africa's Consumer Economy* - www.forbes.com/sites/kevinomarah/2015/01/21/africas-consumer-economy/

— in Africa since 2000.">[5] That last quote is important as far as I'm concerned and points us towards one of the most open and exciting opportunities I believe Africa can present entrepreneurs and businesses right now. But we'll get to that in a moment.

THE CHALLENGE OF PERCEPTION

There is a lot to say about the opportunities Africa offers businesses and entrepreneurs, and there is a lot to say about business from Africa and the amazing innovative spirit it continues to exhibit. But there is also plenty to say about the challenges that face any business looking to penetrate this fantastic continent.

> "Companies can no longer ignore Africa. But they need to manage risks, develop innovative strategies to deal with gaps in infrastructure and training, and recognise that it isn't one market," says McKinsey in a 2011 study.[6]

This sentence presents the first real challenge businesses face: the sheer size and diverse nature of the continent. The World Bank Ease of Doing Business in 2014 put South Africa at 41 while the other four members of BRICS did not do as well (Brazil -- 116; Russia -- 92; India -- 134; China -- 96). Eight African countries were scored ahead of China and Russia, nine ahead of Brazil, and fifteen ahead of India. Yet despite this there is a difficulty in setting up a business across a continent with fifty-four entirely different states each with their own "bureaucratic idiosyncrasies". While setting up in India or China may be more difficult from the outset, the size of the market there means the rewards of

---

5   See Harvard Business Review, *The Globe: Cracking the Next Growth Market: Africa.* Accessed at hbr.org/2011/05/the-globe-cracking-the-next-growth-market-africa

6   See Harvard Business Review, *The Globe: Cracking the Next Growth Market: Africa.* Accessed at hbr.org/2011/05/the-globe-cracking-the-next-growth-market-africa

getting through all the red tape are far bigger than the rewards of setting up in a single African country, and then trying to set up in another and another.

There are also, of course, the challenges around politics and infrastructure. Both of these are not quite what people think, however. Many times one African country's problems are seen to be the entire continent's problems, at least in the public eye. The Ebola outbreaks in 2014 serve as an example of this. The virus broke out in three Western African countries (Liberia, Sierra Leone, Guinea) with a few cases reported in Nigeria. But the response on social media and mainstream Western news channels made one feel as if all of Africa was being swallowed up as a whole, and the rest of the world was next! This is often what happens when a particular African country encounters political turmoil or challenges. The same thing happens with infrastructure. Africa has many large cities that are even more technologically advanced than certain Western cities. But yet, on the whole, the image of a war-torn, dilapidated continent continues to pervade.

Politically there are challenges, but there is also increased stability which has led to the wonderful growth Africa has been enjoying. "The key reasons behind Africa's growth surge were improved political and macroeconomic stability and micro-economic reforms," continues McKinsey in its 2011 Lions on the Move study. What's interesting to me is how technology is actually helping this along.

UNIQUE OPPORTUNITIES
But Africa's real unique business challenges in terms of infrastructure and diversity are also unique opportunities for particular kinds of businesses. "Africa's economic growth is creating sub-

stantial new business opportunities that are often overlooked by global companies," said McKinsey in 2010. The research firm believes that four groups of industries — consumer-facing industries, agriculture, resources, and infrastructure, could together "generate as much as $2.6 trillion in revenue annually by 2020, or $1 trillion more than today." The rate of return on foreign investment in Africa, it continues to say, is higher than in any other developing region. Its recommendation is simple: get in early to create markets, establish your brand, and shape industry structures.

The firm highlights six key sectors that it believes will see the greatest change, and present the greatest opportunity, in Sub-Saharan Africa. I find this interesting as it lines up with many of my own thoughts and spheres of influence. They are: financial services, education, health, retail, agriculture, and government. "Technology-related productivity gains in these sectors could reach $148 billion to $318 billion by 2025, and large populations stand to benefit as a result," says the firm's report. Telecommunications is a wonderful example of a particular kind of niche finding a way to bring products to a unique market, taking advantage of the challenges. As noted earlier, telecom companies have added 316 million subscribers in Africa since 2000, which is more subscribers than the whole of the U.S. population. Since there has been a lack of what we can call traditional infrastructure in Africa for a very long time, new technologies are poised to fill the gap, and they really are doing just that.

In my opinion, mobile technologies are really at the forefront of the opportunity waiting to be harnessed, and the numbers are showing this to be true. Mobile phone penetration is expected to increase by 79 percent by 2020, with mobile broadband connections to reach 160 million by the end of 2016, quadrupling a figure in 2012 from Frost & Sullivan. McKinsey continues to advise in its 2013 report that, "Significant infrastructure investment — for example, increased access to mobile broadband, fibre-optic cable connections to households, and power-supply expansion — combined with the rapid spread of low-cost smartphones and tablets, has enabled millions of Africans to connect for the first time. There is a growing wave of innovation as entrepreneurs and large corporations alike launch new web-based ventures.[7]"

The Internet is able to reduce transaction costs and bring previously unused financial services to people who live far from a bank or ATM. Stats show that more than 60 percent of Africans could have access to banking services by 2025, thanks to new technology, with more than 90 percent using mobile wallets for daily transactions and remittances. This is definitely what has been happening, as we will explore in this book.

In its 2013 report entitled Mobile Insights Study, research group Nielsen summarised its findings this way:

1. More Africans have access to mobile phones than they do clean water.
2. Mobile phone use amongst South African adults rose from just 17% in 2000 to 76% by 2010.
3. More South Africans use mobile phones (29 million) than listen to the radio (28 million) or use a personal computer (6 million).[8]

According to the Africa Telecom and Outlook 2014 report (from

---

7   See McKinsey's report, *Lions go digital: The Internet's transformative potentional in Africa.* Accessed at www.mckinsey.com/insights/high_tech_telecoms_internet/lions_go_digital_the_internets_transformative_potential_in_africa

8   See KPMG, *Looking to the future of telecommunications in South Africa.* Accessed at www.sablog.kpmg.co.za/2013/08/looking-to-the-future-of-telecommunications-in-south-africa/

Informa Telecoms & Media) there were 778 million mobile sub-scriptions in Africa at the end of June 2013 and the continent's mobile-subscription count will reach 1.2 billion by the end of 2018. Mobile data usage and its revenues are growing significantly faster than voice revenues, even from a very low base. This is due to new submarine and terrestrial cables, the roll-out of mobile broadband networks, and the increasing affordability of data services, in addition to economic growth.

It continues:

"As well as facilitating a rise in data connectivity in Africa, these factors are creating a platform for a range of new digital services on the continent, such as mobile financial services [what I call digital payment services], e-commerce and digital content and services for the business market."

This is, for me, where much of the action lies. Technology is constantly evolving, and with it comes new, unique, and out-of-the-box business opportunities that are seeing tremendous results. Things are changing more quickly than most of us realise. There are plenty of aspects to the vast potential of the African continent that are only beginning to emerge as the new technologies emerge. There are new ways of doing business that amazingly revolve around devices we keep in our pocket. Mobile phone technology and the Internet have clearly changed everything about our world, but in Africa the changes are unique and often even surprising. It's even affecting the politics of the continent, creating increased transparency and openness in elections, and allowing for healthy activism to spread. It is not the sole reason for the political stability that Africa is enjoying in many of its quarters, but it has certainly added to it.

Education is being revolutionised, entertainment is taking surprising turns, and agriculture and health are benefiting in tremendous ways. Farmers now have access like never before to weather information, market prices, and apps that even allow for farmers to track their cows' gestation.[9] Text messaging services allow for consumers to know when they are being sold counterfeit medicine, and people can find healthcare solutions at the touch of a button.

All of this has helped to create a new kind of infrastructure where there was none before. In fact, as I said above, the lack of traditional infrastructure is actually creating opportunity and space for the new. We're leapfrogging in surprising areas. Infrastructure now literally sits right in the hands of millions of people. We have computers, telephones, whole volumes of encyclopaedias, millions of newspapers, weather tracking services, banks, whole post offices, and entertainment centres right in our pockets.

The numbers clearly show how Africans are very willing to access all this, provided it is all packaged in a way that Africans find valuable and affordable. That is not proving too difficult, as telecommunication companies can attest to. The current main players have discovered how to do this and cellphone contracts are, by and large, not very expensive, plus there are plenty of pay-as-you-go options. The price of smartphones is dropping significantly too, even worldwide. International Data Corporation (IDC) predicts this will continue and Africa is poised to be one of the biggest consumers of these devices and the benefits that come with them.[10]

---

9   See CNN, *Seven ways mobile phones have changed lives in Africa*. Accessed at edition.cnn. com/2012/09/13/world/africa/mobile-phones-change-africa/

10   See Computerworld, *Smartphone prices are dropping, and will continue to dip through '18*. Accessed at www.computerworld.com/article/2489944/smartphones/smartphone-prices-are-dropping-and-will-continue-to-dip-through--18.html. Also see an IDC press release, accessible at www.idc.com/getdoc.jsp?containerId=prUS25282214

In this book we will be exploring all this in more detail and I am convinced you will find yourself pleasantly surprised.

DIGITAL PAYMENT SERVICES

Let me get some definitions out of the way quickly for easier reading. I refer to all mobile financial services, mobile money and mobile banking, as digital payments. The purists in the financial services world will probably raise an eyebrow at this, but I believe for positioning in the mind of the reader this encapsulates the essence of financial services.

It's in the significant rise of digital payments that my interest lies. Why? Because digital payments underpin access to most of the innovation we see coming out of Africa. What use is pay-as-you-go solar if you can't pay for it? What use is e-learning content if you can't access it?

A colleague of mine encapsulates it so well in this analogy. In presentations at conferences and meetings, he often asks his audience: "What's the most important ingredient in coffee?" Most people chime "Coffee Beans!", "Location it's grown!" etc. He pauses and says, "Water". Digital payments is the water in the coffee of innovation.

Digital payment services are disrupting and revolutionising the market in Africa, where the market never had access to traditional financial services. It's an example of the new coming in because the old simply wasn't there. Farmers now have access to real insurance that they simply could never afford before. Health insurance is a reality for people who could never even have dreamed about it until just a few years ago. In 2012, only one in five people had bank accounts across Sub-Saharan Africa[11]

---

11   See CNN, *Seven ways mobile phones have changed lives in Africa*. Accessed at edition.cnn. com/2012/09/13/world/africa/mobile-phones-change-africa/

but this is changing — and quickly — thanks to the advancement of this new idea. Already we see that 93 percent of Kenya's consumers use mobile phones for banking, while Nigeria is at 85 percent.[12] The point is that as more consumers get their hands on these devices, the more digital payment services will become a focus. I'm convinced this is an exciting, new industry that businesses of all kinds can and must consider. It's not just about banks but all kinds of services, as the micro-insurance success stories later in this book will show us.

So what is this "new idea" of digital payment services? How exactly does it work? How can your industry benefit from it? How should entrepreneurs think about it? How do consumers benefit? Why does Africa, particularly Sub-Saharan Africa, present an amazing opportunity in this realm? How do digital payment services underpin innovation? This is what we will unpack in this book. And as we do, my hope is you will see the tremendous potential of this new industry and see how you can, right now, get on board. If you're an entrepreneur with a keen eye and innovative spirit, you're poised to take advantage of the unique opportunity Africa has to offer, and even change lives for the better through it.

That might seem to be taking it too far, but it's my firm conviction that digital payment services and innovation really can change lives and empower people in ways we've never really seen before. It's a win-win, exciting industry just waiting to be explored.

---

12   See CIO East Africa, *93% of Kenya's consumers using mobile devices for banking.* Accessed at www.cio.co.ke/news/main-stories/93-of-kenya%27s-consumers-using-mobile-devices-for-banking

"The great explosion in private equity, if it is going to occur anywhere around the world in the next couple of years, is probably going to be in Africa, particularly sub-Saharan Africa, where the penetration rate is about one-twelfth or so of what it is in the United States."

—David Rubenstein, CEO of the Carlyle Group

×

CHAPTER TWO

WHY FOCUS ON DIGITAL PAYMENTS IN INNOVATION?

T o understand digital payment services and the amazing benefits of this technology, we must first look at the broader topic of mobile commerce.

Most people think that mobile commerce —the ability to access and use commercial services on your phone —was something Apple invented with the iPhone. While smartphones have changed the game in a big way, mobile commerce has been around for much longer than that. Back in 1997, ten years before the iPhone launched, Kevin Duffey, the managing consultant for Logica's mobile innovation, first coined the term at the launch of the Global Mobile Commerce Forum at Heathrow Hilton in the U.K. He called it "the delivery of electronic commerce capabilities directly into the consumer's hand, anywhere, via wireless technology." He then went on to predict that mobile users would reach 150 million worldwide by the year 2000. He was wrong. There were just under one billion. Fast-forward to 2016 and there are one billion in Africa alone —growing from 500 million in just five years.[13] At the time eyes were on Western Europe, East Asia, Australasia and North America. Africa wasn't even on the radar. But now it has the fastest growing mobile market in the world. In 2015, Nigeria, Ethiopia and Cameroon found themselves among the top ten countries in the world for mobile subscription additions; with a new mobile subscription activated every two seconds in Nigeria.

As you read this you probably have a good idea of how much you use your own phone to purchase items or to at least browse online stores. You might even be reading the e-book version of this book. In 2012, Walmart discovered that 40 percent of visits to its online website were from mobile phones —a number that has probably increased since then. In 2015, 67.1 billion purchases were made from mobile devices by European and U.S. shoppers[14]. U.K. retailers claim that there has been a 31 percent increase (between 2013 —2014) in revenue thanks to the convenience of the mobile phone.

One of the first experiments in the idea of mobile commerce came, interestingly enough, from experimenting with vending machines in Finland which accepted payment via SMS. The project was revolutionary. The Merita Bank of Finland liked the idea and thus created the first mobile phone-based banking service, which made use of SMS technology. Companies in Finland saw the benefits quite quickly and Finnair were the first airline to create a mobile check-in system.

To pay and download digital content from a mobile phone was the obvious next step, and that took place the very next year. As

---

13   See AfricaOutlook, *Ericsson Mobility Report: Connecting the Unconnected.* Accessed at www.africaoutlookmag.com/news/ericsson-mobility-report-connecting-the-unconnected

14   See Bank of America, *Trends in Consumer Mobility Report,* available at newsroom.bankofamerica.com/files/doc_library/additional/2015_BAC_Trends_in_Consumer_Mobility_Report.pdf

you can see, this was long before we could buy music off iTunes. Interestingly enough, music was the catalyst — ringtones were the first item you could buy and download to your phone.

In 1999 two other approaches emerged which set the platform for the technology today. Smart Money,[15] an electronic wallet, was launched in the Philippines. Using SMS, people could pay bills, reload airtime, and transfer money. In Japan, i-Mode was launched, giving users access to services over their phone such as email, sports results, games, weather services, ticket booking and, of course, financial services. It made use of a revenue-sharing model which has also set the pace for many of today's models.

As SMS technology developed it became more possible for more sophisticated services such as mobile ticketing, purchasing, and business applications. Soon consumers could buy airline and train tickets, or concert tickets, or pay for parking or do any number of things from their mobile phone.

BUT NOW THE SMARTPHONE

The trouble with SMS, however, is that it has bottlenecks and many security problems. The good thing about it is, however, that it's much more widely accessible. But the smartphone has allowed for solutions to the problems and to increase the general experience with push-notifications, location-based service, scanning services, track-your-order online services, and apps. Traditional 'bricks and mortar' stores are integrating their online experiences with their stores, allowing for notifications of flash sales, or for consumers to even scan items at the store using their phone and read reviews, or receive coupons via email or the app and use these in the stores, or simply buy with a solution like SnapScan (which we will look at later in this book). Many of these cam-

---

15   See *What is Smart Money?* from SMART. smart.com.ph/Money/what-is-smart-money

paigns have helped to increase profitability in stores.

In his very influential book, The Innovator's Dilemma, the business academic Clayton M. Christensen speaks about the crossroads where technology companies must either decide to carry on with the strategies that have had them enjoy success, or make a big, sudden change that takes into account the shifting market. The truth is that markets are always shifting. And businesses need to shift.

Banking, for example, is one area that needs a shift for two reasons: (1) Its present model is not reaching the lower markets; (2) even developed markets are changing. But it's not just banking that needs to change, but financial services in general, if financial inclusion of the world's poor (and the massive opportunities this provides) is to become a reality. The amazing spin-off of the change we're seeing right now is that other kinds of services are seeing the potential, too.

It goes without saying that, these days, a mobile phone is much more convenient than a laptop or even a tablet, and it is the technology of choice for most people, regardless of where they live. Common sense tells us there is a great future here. But the retail side of things tends to get the greater airtime when there is far more going on —and that 'far more' is in the realm of digital payment services. Here we are seeing major innovation to the way we've done things in the past. Companies like M-Pesa in Kenya, or Fidor Bank, or even Bitcoin are making us think of money —and the way we handle it —very differently. We are seeing innovation in not only technology but the way we sell insurance, do our banking, make our payments, approach education and health services, and much, much more. It's not just about new markets or shifting markets, but a very paradigm shift in the way our world is working.

This is what digital payments services is about —having the world's financial services in the palm of your hand. It's key to financial inclusion. Tomorrow's banks might be providing the world with loans and insurance while only having one physical branch, with trillions of branches on every mobile phone across the world. Or, perhaps, even no branch at all. It's happening already —the U.K. based Atom Bank, launched in 2016, has no branches, but works through its app only. "I personally believe the banking industry is ripe for disruption. It's opaque, or worse than opaque. It's deliberately confusing," says Mark Mullen, CEO of Atom Bank, who previously worked for HSBC. So far, the bank has raised £135 million in funding. I'm eagerly waiting to see what happens, because Africa is ripe for this sort of thing (as you will see in this book).

In other words it's not just a mobile device any more, it's a fully-fledged store or branch of every single company and service in the world, all in your pocket.

So, let's unpack how this all fits together.

"I actually believe that Africa is at the stage that Asia was 15 odd years ago. Where a number of companies viewed Asia as a real opportunity to plant flags and grow, aggressively. And I think Africa is at that stage… Those of us that can go local, and plant ourselves properly, with the right investment, the right quality of people locally, and the right technology transfer, we can win a lot in Africa."

—Ajay Banga, President and CEO of Mastercard

×

CHAPTER THREE

AFRICA — A LAND OF CHALLENGES AND OPPORTUNITY

I n the first century the Roman, Pliny the Elder, wrote down a famous saying at the time: "Ex Africa semper aliquid novi!" (Something new always comes out of Africa). This was said in a negative way, in the context of some very strange ideas on what African people were like. But today this phrase has a new context, a new meaning, and it's a positive one.

Africa has remained surprisingly buoyant since the 2008 recession, seeing global businesses take more and more interest in the continent, especially as its overall GDP is outrunning the rest of the world. There are plenty of new opportunities here —oil and gas, tourism, and, as noted by Investec, "huge growth in mobile banking and mobile technology". With "steadier exchange rates, robust commodity prices, increased private capital flows and modest inflation,"[16] there is a lot to talk about.

But there are challenges, and how you look at them is a great

---

16   See Investec, *Africa: Continent of Opportunities and Challenges*. Accessed at www.investec. co.za/content/dam/investec/investec-international/documents/PIF/Forward-Curve/2014-06/ AS-EN-FS-africa-continent-of-opportunities-and-challenges-25-06-2014.pdf

measure of your entrepreneurial muscle. Issues in infrastructure such as power (the Eskom crisis in South Africa is a great
example), transport, health, clean sanitation and water, and
agricultural challenges are all worth talking about. These are
all a challenge for businesses looking to come to Africa, but also
unique opportunities. Patience, persistence, and a fair dose of
out-of-the-box thinking is required.

> As noted by Investec, "What is clear is that successful
> African infrastructure development requires a 'bottom-up'
> approach, where the ultimate infrastructure service is
> affordable and meets local needs over the longer term."[17]
> And this is exactly where digital payment services comes in.
> I'll quote Investec again: "This requires the close involvement
> of local development partners and funders who can suc-
> cessfully navigate the operating environment and ensure
> that the ultimate infrastructure solution meets the needs of
> its African users."

As we will see throughout this book, when innovators do exactly
that, things start getting exciting.

SUCCESS STORIES AND EXAMPLES

In 2013, Kenya suffered a nationwide power blackout, which
—thanks to a power surge in Nairobi —completely fried many
electronic devices. This was, of course, a disaster for many people
and companies and is an infrastructure problem common to
Africa. But this challenge led to Kenya-based company Ushahidi

---

17 See Investec, Africa: Continent of Opportunities and Challenges. Accessed at
www.investec.co.za/content/dam/investec/investec-international/documents/PIF/For-
ward-Curve/2014-06/AS-EN-FS-africa-continent-of-opportunities-and-challenges-25-06-2014.
pdf

(Swahili for 'testimony') to come up with a unique and interesting product —a surge-resistant, self-powered mobile Wi-Fi router which provides a steady data connection even when the power is out, or if you're out in the middle of nowhere.

> "We realised that what we really needed was a smart, rugged device that could connect to the internet any way it could, hop from one network to another, create a hotspot for multiple devices, while plugged in or running on battery power," says the company.

So they set out to redesign connectivity for the world they live in — Africa. Such a device needed to be physically robust, able to connect to multiple networks, and a hub for all local devices, and have enough backup power to survive a blackout. Due to the changing way that the world is connecting to the web (most of us don't first access the Internet through our desktop) and the way we're constantly on the move, it had to be something easily mobile.

So they designed the BRCK, for cafe-hoppers in San Francisco to struggling coders in Nairobi, as they like to put it. As explained by one of the founders, Erik Hersman, it's a "backup generator for the Internet".

The device also collects weather data, creates secure networks wherever you set it up, and you can perform remote repairs via the cloud. The first 700 to buy the product came from 45 different countries. It is assembled in the U.S, even though the company says people in the U.S. or Europe don't understand it. "But anyone who lives in the emerging markets," says Hersman, "their question is 'When do I get to buy it?'"

Ushahidi are no strangers to innovation either. In 2008, out of post-election violence in Kenya, it designed a crowdsourcing mapping platform which collated eyewitness reports of violence, either sent in via email or text message, and then placed these on Google maps so everyone could know what was going on. Harvard's Kennedy School of Government found that the system was better than the media at reporting violence and keeping people informed. Now, the software is also used to help track pharmacy stockouts in South East Africa, and has been used to monitor elections in several other countries (including Mexico and India). Italy uses it to manage forest fires, Australia and the U.S. to map floods, and the Asia-Pacific region uses it for disaster management training events — and these are just a few examples.

We can learn two lessons from the story of this company. Firstly, that technology innovation is indeed coming from Africa, and being used across the world. Secondly that we don't have to rely on traditional infrastructure. Here, the lack of traditional infrastructure is driving the innovation, creating new kinds of infrastructure in Africa that will make it a very different world in the future to the developed nations of today. A very good world. There is money to be made from this technology for entrepreneurs who are looking. As said by Deo Onyango, a General Electric executive from Kenya, "There are ideas that could be built out of Africa that we don't know yet."

M-Kopa Kenya Ltd. is another example of how innovation can sell to what some call "the bottom billion". It essentially sells pay-as-you-go solar power —a solar panel with a prepaid meter. People who live in rural areas far away from traditional power infrastructure can pay a deposit for the solar panel and pay as they use it every day, through micro-payments using the M-Pesa mobile phone payment system (which we will look at in more detail in the next chapter) until they have paid for the solar panel.

This is an example of digital payment services working to enhance people's lives and create new kinds of infrastructure. The pay-as-you-go price is less than what it costs to buy fuel for a kerosene lamp, which is what most people would use. Then, once the solar panel is paid for —which usually takes a year —the users enjoy free electricity. Not only is it cheaper than having to use kerosene, but it is also safer as kerosene's fumes are harmful.

SCAN THE QR CODE TO LISTEN TO HOW PAY-AS-YOU-GO SOLAR POWER IS TAKING OFF IN AFRICA.

In a similar vein, Patrick Ngowi saw an opportunity in Tanzania's power infrastructure and realised a solution lay in solar —all it needed was an effective distribution channel. So he started Helvetic Solar Contractors, which is expanding beyond Tanzania now as well.

"Being an African owned company with extensive on-ground experience, we apply a robust rural and urban product distribution model incorporating a network of over 98 registered re-sellers of our solar products and services throughout East Africa. Helvetic Solar is the leading Pan-African solar company with online and mobile platform addressing all solar power and solar thermal needs from unit to project level," says the over 8-million in revenues company.

Nigerian Jason Njoku is another example. He saw how much Internet connectivity was growing in Africa (according to Internet World Stats, more than 15 percent of Africa's population has access to the Internet —167 million are online, with 50 million of those on Facebook) and saw an entertainment opportunity by getting the "Nollywood" film industry online, now delivering content to more than 500,000 customers worldwide through his iROKOtv service, and helping to boost the entertainment industry in Africa. (Nollywood is the world's second largest film industry in terms of income per capita, employing more than 300,000 people.)

In this book I feature quite a number of entrepreneurs, but I have also tried as much as possible to feature intrapreneurs (an employee in an organisation who promotes innovative product development). One of such intrapreneurs is Muhammad Nana, whom on his own accord assisted the #OperationHydrate programme in January 2016 in South Africa to raise over R60 million (approximately $4 million) in a weekend. #OperationHydrate rallied up South Africans to donate water to drought affected areas — with particular PR exposure via Twitter. But the only way for South Africans to donate was via a bank transfer. As you can imagine, this would have been quite clunky and thus donation opportunities could be lost. So Muhammad implemented a social media link which South Africans could click on and then have their bank's MasterPass App pop up, allowing for donation to be done in seconds! I was thoroughly impressed by this and featured him on the show as our first intrapreneur. I've got no doubt that Nana will soon become the social digital payments guru in South Africa. All you have to do is spend an afternoon with him and you'll buy into his vision for social payments.

These are wonderful stories, but I would like to draw your attention to a trend here. To access all these services you need to be able to pay for them. Digital payment services is key for the success of these innovations; water to our innovation coffee.

IT'S CHANGING

As Bill Clinton has said, in speaking of Africa, "Intelligence, dreams and the willingness to work are evenly distributed throughout the world." While certain infrastructure and systems allow for dreams to flourish, and others make it difficult, the reality is that things are changing. And as we shall see in this book, examples abound in many other industries as well, and all of these have some kind of link to digital payments. It's all interconnected. Digital payment services even have something to bring to the entertainment industry, the health industry, and education! We'll cover all of these. But the point I want to highlight here is the entrepreneurial spirit of Africa.

"Sub-Saharan Africa is also a region with the highest rate of adults involved in early-stage entrepreneurial activity. The entrepreneurial activity occurring in this area is over two times that of North America (11 percent) and over three times that of Europe (8 percent). This means that approximately 27 percent of adults (ages 18-64) in Sub-Saharan Africa are involved in start-up businesses," says the Huffington Post's Aurora Chisté.[18] Isn't that interesting?

Multinational businesses are seeing the innovation coming from Africa and getting on board. When you look at the kind of

---

18   See Huffington Post, *West Africa: Transforming Potential into Impact.* Accessed at www. huffingtonpost.com/aurora-chiste/west-africa-transforming- b 6575132.html

funding that's coming from these, it should make you ask some great questions. International Business Machines Corps. has set up a research facility in Nairobi just to find technology solutions to African problems. Microsoft helps entrepreneurs with registering intellectual property, while General Electric Co. is investing heavily into inventors with what it calls its GE Garages.

Seven out of the ten fastest growing economies in the world are in Africa. Democracy in Sub-Saharan Africa has grown from three countries to twenty-five in the last twenty-five years, and "there is a growing middle class", says the Milken Institute. The International Monetary Fund's (IMF) World Economic Outlook for 2013 included economic growth for 185 countries and, out of these, it selected twenty with the highest projected compounded annual growth rate (CAGR) from 2013 through 2017. Out of these twenty there were none from the West but all were from Africa and Asia.

DIGITAL PAYMENT SERVICES IN AFRICA

This now brings me to digital payment services specifically in Africa. We've already seen a case example above of how digital payment services have impacted Africans in Kenya, with the M-Pesa service in particular. While we'll look at M-Pesa specifically in the next chapter, we're currently getting an overview of digital payment successes —and opportunities.

Digital payment services are, quite simply, changing the tide in Sub-Saharan Africa when it comes to financial inclusion. While only two percent of adults worldwide make use of mobile money accounts, that number is twelve percent in Sub-Saharan Africa. Sub-Saharan Africa houses all thirteen of the countries in the world where more than ten percent of the population owns a mobile money account. East Africa sees up to twenty percent of adults having a mobile money account, while ten percent actually have a mobile money account only and no other bank account. More specifically, in Cote d'Ivoire, Somalia, Tanzania, Uganda, and Zimbabwe, more adults have a mobile money account than at any other kind of bank. Kenya, for reasons we shall see, takes the largest share of this, but other countries of interest are Somalia, Tanzania, and Uganda.

All the fundamentals for robust economics currently points to Africa's favour. We're seeing better, and more consistent, exchange rates; robust commodity prices; increased private capital; and modest inflation. "We wouldn't be investing as much in the rest of Africa if we didn't believe Africa will be the success story in the next decades… Africa is on the move and it is moving forward," says Julian Roberts, Old Mutual Group Chief Executive.[19] Urbanisation is increasing and there is a steady rise of the middle class. But the beauty of digital payment services is that it appeals to all classes. A World Bank-Gallup poll in 2015 shows that the gap between the rich and the poor having a bank account in Kenya and Tanzania simply does not exist when it comes to the two having mobile financial accounts. This means that not only the poor see the benefit in digital payment services. But as McKinsey says, it's worth looking at the lower income market in Africa. "The 3.7 billion people living on less than $3 a day represent a $5 trillion dollar market." However you may think of C. K. Prahalad's well-known book, The Fortune at the Bottom of the Pyramid, this is worth thinking about.

And what we shall see, and this is where things are turned on their head, is that it's not only digital payment services that are attracting the world's unbanked in Africa. For example, the

---

19 See Forbes, *Top Quotes About Africa At The 2014 World Economic Forum In Davos.* Accessed at www.forbes.com/sites/faraigundan/2014/01/28/top-quotes-about-africa-at-the-2014-world-economic-forum-in-davos/#7d2a32455df5

solar system mentioned above is a huge catalyst for uptake on the M-Pesa service. New Findex data and CGAP, in particular, are looking at this space closely. It's all interconnected. As Melinda and Bill Gates have stated, "We think the next 15 years will see major breakthroughs for most people in poor countries… These breakthroughs will be driven by innovation in technology — ranging from new vaccines and hardier crops to much cheaper smartphones and tablets — and by innovations that help deliver those things to more people."

HOW IT'S CHANGING IN THE WEST

It may be that Africa, and Kenya in particular, was the starting point for true digital payment services, and the developed world is just catching up. However, it's catching up fast. And as things progress in the developed world so they will progress significantly in the developing world, and eventually vice versa. The African-based digital payment service of M-Pesa has begun to extend its reach into Eastern Europe. Ross McEwan, CEO of the Royal Bank of Scotland, provides one quote that highlights how things are changing: "Our busiest branch in 2014 is the 7:01 from Reading to Paddington —over 167,000 of our customers use our Mobile Banking app between 7am and 8am on their commute to work every day." Other banks, such as HBOS (part of Lloyd's Banking Group) stated at a 2015 conference that many of its customers were using mobile banking only — not a branch, or call centre, or even Internet banking, but solely and only through the mobile app. The 2015 Bank of America Trends in Consumer Mobility Report[20] highlights that 51 percent of Americans make use of mobile or Internet banking as their primary method. Meanwhile,

---

20   See *Trends in Consumer Mobility Report*. Accessed at newsroom.bankofamerica.com/files/ doc_library/additional/2015_BAC_Trends_in_Consumer_Mobility_Report.pdf

the 2015 North America Consumer Banking Survey[21] shows us that 81 percent of consumers would not be bothered at all if their local bank branch closed, because they can access everything they need via mobile.

The growth of mobile banking is exponentially faster than Internet banking. According to the Market Intelligence Strategy Centre, it took three years for mobile banking in Australia to reach well over six million, while it took four years for that number to be reached for Internet banking. But that's nothing compared to Barclays Bank which states that, "It took 13 years to get two million customers using Internet banking; it took just two months to reach that number for mobile banking."

In 2014 it appeared that the tide turned. Chris Skinner, one of the world's best experts in digital banking, noted in a 2015 survey that bankers no longer see mobile as an emerging technology but now as a mainstream channel. Innovation in the retail space is now much higher on the agenda than before.[22] This is especially the case with Apple and Google moving into the payments space.

So there is a lot to be said for how things are changing. But before we get into thinking in more detail about how to tap into the market, it would be good to look at some success cases in particular.

21   See Accenture, *North America Consumer Digital Banking Survey 2015*. Accessed at www. accenture.com/us-en/insight-consumer-banking-survey.aspx

22   See Chris Skinner's blog, *The Changing Face of Payments*. Accessed at thefinanser.co.uk/ fsclub/2015/06/the-changing-face-of-payments-free-research-report.html

"Africans... are way ahead of us in many ways with the use of technology. They have skipped over the non-existent telephone (wired) network to use cellular and are bypassing the erratic and sometimes non-existent electric grid by increasingly harnessing solar energy. The use of these technologies is bringing otherwise remote communities and peoples together, and opening avenues for commerce and banking."
—Vivian Gast, President of Non-Profit "Earth Wind & Fire" and Project Coordinator of Ndabibi Environmental Conservation Centre, Kenya

CHAPTER FOUR

KENYA — AN INNOVATION SUCCESS

I really did struggle to find innovation stories for my radio slot that didn't come out of Kenya. It seems innovation is in the very fabric of the Kenyan society. Their most renowned innovation, in Africa and across the world, is M-Pesa. M-Pesa ('pesa' is Swahili for 'money'), operated by Safaricom (Kenya's largest mobile operator) and Vodafone, it's a mobile phone money transfer and microfinancing service that has seen huge success. It was originally established in 2007 and has since expanded into other African countries, India, and Eastern Europe.

So much has been said and written about M-Pesa — a simple Google search yields tons of results. But for purposes of positioning innovation and digital payments, I thought it prudent to include a chapter on it here.

The system is surprisingly simple. Basically, your phone becomes your bank and ATM. You can deposit money into your account, receive money from others into it, and, of course, pay from it. You can even draw cash from it by using a participating agent. And unlike a traditional bank you're not paying monthly fees or deposit fees (but of course, there are transaction fees, which are actually quite affordable). It is effectively branchless, digital banking. In 2010 M-Pesa was noted as the most successful digital payment service in the developing world. In 2012 it grew to 17 million M-Pesa accounts being active, in 2014 it was 19 million. And it continues to grow exponentially. Many have praised the service for providing financial systems to millions of people who otherwise could not afford it, while also reducing crime since less people are carrying around cash.

According to Alan Cassels of DHL, Kenya has actually become the birthplace of mobile banking when M-Pesa was introduced back in 2007. "This has transformed the way business is done. M-Pesa can be used for paying taxis, paying duties on import shipments or paying a friend. It also means people carry less cash, which can lead to a reduction in crime." Calling it the 'birthplace' of mobile banking isn't strictly correct, but it has certainly been the birthplace of a highly successful model that has surpassed the experiments happening in Norway and Japan before.

> "It is like magic," says The Economist.[23] "By clicking a few keys on a mobile phone, money can be zapped from one part of Kenya to another in seconds. For urban migrants sending money home to their villages, and for people used to queuing at banks for hours to pay bills or school fees, the M-Pesa money-transfer service… is a godsend."

The numbers are staggering, although admittedly sometimes difficult to discern. Some statistics say that M-Pesa contributes

---

23   See the Economist, *Out of Thin Air*. Accessed at www.economist.com/node/16319635

up to 43 percent of Kenya's GDP.[24]

CGAP has made an attempt to make sense of many of the numbers:

"First, the value of mobile money transactions quoted includes all aggregate flows both into and out of the mobile money system — so at the very least this statistic is double counting. More importantly, GDP is a measure of the value of goods and services an economy produces and does not represent the amount of money that had to flow through it to pay for these goods and services. In actuality, M-Pesa flows are roughly equal to the transaction flows of one of Kenya's larger commercial banks. According to the Central Bank, mobile money contributes to 6.59% of the total national payments throughput value (including both gross and retail) but a staggering 66.56% of the total NPS throughput volume. This means that M-Pesa is important, but does not necessarily pose a systemic risk. However, M-Pesa's reach across all economic segments of Kenyans, coupled with its high usage for financial transactions, means that the product's security can influence public perceptions of safety and security of financial transactions."[25]

Whether the numbers are exactly right, or not, the fact is that a branchless bank is enjoying profitability akin to a traditional bank —without the costs involved. The fact is, also, that this branchless bank is able to much more easily expand to other countries. And

24   See Forbes, *M-Pesa and the Rise of the Global Money Market*. Accessed at www.forbes.com/ sites/danielrunde/2015/08/12/m-pesa-and-the-rise-of-the-global-mobile-money-market/#22f-baea023f5

25   See CGAP, *10 Myths about M-Pesa: 2014 Update*. Accessed at www.cgap.org/blog/10-myths-about-m-pesa-2014-update

this is key: it's changing people's perceptions about finance and financial institutions.

HOW DOES IT WORK, EXACTLY?

The way it works is simple: you simply SMS the amount you want to send (to a friend or an account or for a utility bill) and they can spend it at participating stores or withdraw cash from participating agents or a local participating M-Pesa office. It's kind of like PayPal, in a basic sense, except it is much more versatile. This all happens without hefty bank fees and using something people already have, and are actually more keen to invest in than a bank account: a mobile phone.

The coupling of this service with mobile operators is a win-win situation. By incentivising people not only with a mobile bank account but also with extra talk-time minutes or the like, people are much more likely to invest. M-Pesa has now expanded beyond Kenya, operating in Tanzania, Afghanistan, South Africa, India, Fiji, DRC, Eastern Europe, Mozambique, Lesotho, and Egypt.[26] In Uganda, DHL's Asteway Desta notes: "Banks are now differentiating themselves through what they can do in terms of automation. They are constantly encouraging electronic banking and incentivising customers to do so."[27]

In addition to the millions of person-to-person (P2P) and customer-to-business (C2B) transactions, there are also other real-world incentives as more industries and service providers learn how to make use of this service. For example, in Kenya, Water Company customers are even using use M-Pesa to buy

---

26   See Vodafone's website at www.vodafone.com/content/index/about/about-us/money transfer.html. Accessed October, 2015.

27   See How We Made It In Africa, *How technology is changing the way business is being done in Africa.* Accessed at www.howwemadeitinafrica.com/how-technology-is-changing-the-way-business-is-being-done-in-africa/45821/

credits which they receive on their phone, and which they can use to pay for clean, fresh water when they need it. One of the poorer areas in the capital of Nairobi, Mathare, serves as an example. Clean water is not readily available and people generally have to use expensive vendors to get their drinking water. Residents have a smart card which they can top up their credits on their smart-phone and then swipe at an ATM-like dispenser, which provides them clean water.

The cost is significantly cheaper. The BBC's Ahmed Adan reported in the suburb of Eastleigh that vendors are selling water at 50 Kenya shillings for 20 litres —100 times the price at the new water dispensing machines.[28] Clean drinking water is one of the United Nations' Millenium Development Goals, and it's been estimated that more than 700 million people do not have access to it. This is a step in the right direction, set up by a Danish water-company Grundfos in partnership with local government. It is a public-private partnership model which Grundfos believes can be developed well in other countries too.

Mobile micro-insurance is another very interesting develop-ment, which I've given a chapter all on its own. So is the growth of agri-business apps. M-Pesa's partnership with agri-business company M-Farm Limited has increased transparency in the market with the sharing of crop prices, training resources, and an exchange platform for commodities. "This software will ensure that farmers are no longer exploited by middlemen who make away with all the profits leaving the small scale farmers with little if any income," says Jamilla Abbas, M-Farm CEO.

Mobile is the main way people in Africa access the Internet and, thus, the world. It has taken banks a long time to see the

---

28   See the BBC, *Kenya slum Mathare gets cheap water through ATMs.* Accessed at www.bbc. com/news/world-africa-33223922

potential in mobile, and in Kenya they may actually be too late! Chris Skinner travels the world speaking and convincing banks that there is a future in digital banking. One can say that, in many ways, banks have been almost forced to accept the change of technology in the last few years. If they had their way they might have preferred for it to have been business as usual, while remaining frustrated at the fact that they were making no inroads to financial inclusion amongst the lower income groups. M-Pesa, however, can offer a bridge —one which the aforementioned Atom Bank (mentioned in chapter 2) are probably very interested in.

M-Pesa's success has been a precursor for many other services and ideas. Its success even made the World Bank, in 2012, issue a monopoly warning about the way payment systems are developing, citing M-Pesa as an example![29] M-Pesa has largely dominated Kenya, but there is competition —and there is lots of competition in neighbour countries. Tanzania is one such example, which we'll look at next, as the method and way in which digital payment services have seen success there is quite different.

---

29   See The Wall Street Journal, *Is African Mobile Money Becoming Too Successful?* Accessed at blogs.wsj.com/tech-europe/2012/07/23/is-african-mobile-money-becoming-too-successful/

"Africa has become the big game of the nation hunters. Today, Africa looms as the greatest commercial, industrial and political prize in the world."
—Marcus Garvey, Jamaican Politician, Entrepreneur

CHAPTER FIVE

TANZANIA — PROVING THAT WE CAN COLLABORATE

Tanzania is another success story when it comes to digital payment services, with unprecedented growth from 2010 to 2015, but interestingly the path to success was very different.

In 2008 less than one percent of Tanzanian adults had access to mobile financial services, but this shot up to 90 percent by 2013. The country enjoys over 38 million mobile money accounts in 2015 (just 4.2 million in 2009). There are over 95 million transactions every month on Tanzanian mobile money services, which is actually more than Kenya. These are fantastic numbers for a market that only a few years ago was being seen as a write-off for digital payment services.

Customer expectations in Tanzania for digital payment services are very positive. GSMA, a trade organisation representing the interests of mobile operators globally, conducted a survey in 2015 which shows that 87 percent of those surveyed viewed digital payment services as cheaper, 83 percent as quicker, 82 percent as easier to use, 78 percent as safer, and 75 percent as more convenient. 51 percent of respondents paid and received money using a digital payments service, compared to the next most popular method of hand-delivery, which sits at only 23 percent. Only two percent reported that they conduct direct deposits into bank accounts.

While M-Pesa truly dominates the market in Kenya, the Tanzanian market is much more competitive, and this has been a strategic move by both the government and the private sector. It was realised that interoperability is key, and the outcome of this realisation came into effect in a very practical way in September 2014, when customers in one digital payment service could finally transfer money to someone else in a different digital payment service. Studies showed that customers were mostly in favour of such a service (up to 90 percent of customers said they would make use of such a service, says International Finance Corporation (IFC).[30] After all, we can do it with traditional banking, why not digital payment services?

I was very privileged when the Executives of Tigo Tanzania, Andrew Hodgson & Tariq Dhiyebi, kept punting the concept of interoperability at a conference I was chairing. It was a very radical concept at the time, and even more impressive was that only two years later they had successfully implemented interoperability with all the operators in Tanzania. Because more than half of the providers of digital payment services in Tanzania work with several providers, customers now have more choice and more convenience. If a competitor offers something better it's not difficult to switch. Customers receive all sorts of benefits from many other services tied into digital payment services, such as micro-insurance. The service providers encourage competi-

---

30   See IFC's Case Study, *Achieving Interoperability In Mobile Financial Services*. Accessed at www.ifc.org/wps/wcm/connect/8d518d004799ebf1bb8fff299ede9589/IFC+Tanzania+Case+-study+10_03_2015.pdf?MOD=AJPERES

tion which is creating interesting product offerings and new ways to get into the market.

AN UNPRECEDENTED MOVE

What I find even more fascinating is customers are now also offered interest on their mobile money accounts. Tigo Tanzania has been a front-runner in this space. In September 2014, right as interoperability began, it also began to return interest generated on its trust account to users — $8.7 million (USD) was given to 3.5 million users, and then a further $1.8 million in November. Tigo stated that it plans to make such reimbursements every quarter. The result was a net inflow of cash of 11 percent, says GSMA's study cited below,[31] and an increase in the volume of transactions.

> "For many customers, the pay-out represents a substantial sum relative to their monthly income. According to Tigo, for the past three and a half years the Tigo Pesa Trust Fund has been able to achieve a return of between 5 — 12% and aims to achieve a competitive rate in future. Tigo plans to return all of this money back to its customers. With inflation in Tanzania running just over 6%, this represents a significant return on customers' investment in mobile money," says the study.

Tigo's upshot is an increase in the money customers will keep in their accounts. Tigo isn't looking for people to see this as an investment account, but is looking to garner their 'under the mattress' cash savings. This is a very interesting reality and creates a new

---

31   See GSMA's *2014 State of the Industry: Mobile Financial Services for the Unbanked.* Accessed at www.gsma.com/mobilefordevelopment/wp-content/uploads/2015/03/SOTIR_2014.pdf

way of thinking of financial inclusion. Tigo has also managed another global first by launching cross-border remittances to and from Rwanda. Other providers are also now creating mobile credit services, which we look at in more detail in the chapter on banking.

GOVERNMENT & PRIVATE PARTNERSHIP

The situation in Tanzania has been helped greatly by smart regulation from the Bank of Tanzania (BOT), which sees digital payment services as absolutely key in financial inclusion. BOT's approach has been to let the private sector lead the way with a "test and learn" approach. I think it's actually brilliant. The private sector jumped on board with commercial banks soon enhancing their partnerships with mobile financial services.

> "We have learned that new technologies that augur well with the Central Bank's objective need to be nurtured and monitored closely to ensure they do not cause any financial instability or reputational risk that may affect the country's payment systems. This approach has made digital payment services in Tanzania a success story," says Prof Benno Ndulu, governor of Bank of Tanzania.

This kind of partnership is obviously now being replicated in other countries too. The GSMA has noted this in its own study, highlighting that several banks and MNOs have formed partnerships to launch individual savings products tailored to the needs of mobile money users. Commercial Bank of Africa and Safaricom's M-Shwari service in Kenya, and Steward Bank and Econet's EcoSave service in Zimbabwe, serve as examples. "There are also several financial institution/bank-led dedicated mobile saving services, which are paired to the provider's mobile money services. These include Nationwide Microbank's MiCash in Papua New Guinea, Housing Finance Bank's mcash in Uganda and Bank Sinar's Sinar Sip in Indonesia," says the GSMA.

The government of Tanzania has seen how digital payment services can truly help its citizens. For example, medical care. Because of the high cost of travel, many patients can't get to the medical care they need. But Comprehensive Community Based Rehabilitation in Tanzania (CCBRT), an NGO, is now able to easily send money to patients through digital payment services which they can use to pay for their travel. Plus, there are some seriously cool developments in this sphere, which will cover in the next chapter.

INTERCONNECTION

We can now begin to see how digital payment services and other industries and services can interconnect. In addition to the health sector, which we will look at next, I've selected other key industries and sectors to showcase how digital payment services can truly change people's lives. These include education, insurance, banking, entertainment, agriculture, transport and banking. In each of these, innovation has come from Africa by Africans. These are only examples, too, and I don't pretend that I am providing an exhaustive list. I believe digital payment services can ultimately bring something to every sector and industry. This will all become clearer, and more exciting, as we continue to unpack innovation.

"For tomorrow belongs to the people who prepare for it today."

—**An african proverb**

CHAPTER SIX

DISRUPTING
THE HEALTH SECTOR

E very year, uncounted lives are lost because of a lack of information on health. Many expecting moms in rural villages simply don't know what to expect from their pregnancy, how to ensure their pregnancy goes well, and don't know when things are going wrong. Even the most basic of services or information can truly save lives.

It's not only the information coming to people, but the information going to doctors, hospitals, and medical personnel who can help. Mobile devices are opening up the ability for information to flow both of these ways quickly, efficiently, and cheaply, making healthcare more affordable. If an infectious disease breaks out in a remote area it can take too long for those who can make a difference to even find out. By the time the data is collected and understood and received by decision-makers the outbreak could have already become an epidemic.

But real-time data can be collected and sent to the right people through mobile phone technologies. And data can be sent back to patients, giving them advice and information. One thinks of Star Trek's "tricorder" device, which scans the body and then makes recommendations, sending information to the doctor in real-time, which is actually not that far-fetched these days. Other devices such as the upcoming Scanadu device[32] and wearable computing are all in line with this sort of idea.

This new approach to health has been dubbed mHealth (Mobile Health). It's part of a larger category called eHealth, which refers to using computers and information technology for different health services. MHealth has the potential to dramatically reduce death and disease, as well as help fight the growing counterfeit medicine industry, prevent medicine stock-outs, and overall improve the health of individuals. If you think I'm being a bit over-the-top with such statements, let me show you what I mean.

While developed nations can certainly find a benefit, this is becoming another one of those cases where the lack of traditional infrastructure in developing nations is causing the rise of a totally different kind of infrastructure, due to the consistently rapid rise in mobile phone penetration. According to Berg Insight, a market research firm, in 2012, about 2.8 million patients around the world were using some kind of home monitoring service with equipment that uses data connectivity in some way. The firm forecasted that this would grow at a compound annual growth rate (CAGR) of 26.9 percent by 2017, eventually reaching 9.4 million connections globally by the end of that forecast period. It added that the number of these devices that have integrated cellular connectivity increased from 0.73 million in 2011 to about 1.03 million in 2012, and is projected to grow at a CAGR of 46.3 percent to 7.10 million in 2017.[33] Smartphone apps in this space

---

32   See www.scanadu.com/

33   See M2M Research Study, *mHealth and Home Monitoring*. Accessed at www.berginsight. com/reportpdf/productsheet/bi-mhealth5-ps.pdf

are becoming increasingly available, and there are estimates that say that about 500 million patients used these apps in 2015.

Examples abound and, like with most of mobile technology, it starts with SMS. A study conducted from May 2007 to October 2008 showed just how effective text messaging could be in the fight against HIV. HIV patients who lived in remote areas were sent a weekly text message in their local language asking them how they were feeling. If no response was received within 48 hours, a healthcare worker would call and would visit if it was required. The study also put patients in a control group with no text messaging.

"The result was that 63 per cent of mobile phone users reported treatment adherence; compared with only 50 per cent in the control group. Viral loads were undetectable in 57 per cent of patients who received the weekly text messages compared with 48 per cent in the control group," reports Scidev.net.[34]

One of the other benefits is systems. New technology makes sharing information between systems easier, which is paramount. This is especially important these days because, since the 90's, data systems have been quite fragmented (this was partly the result of a rising range of donors in global health since that time). The new mobile technology, however, is much more open and uses the same standards across the board. This is quite an overlooked, but brilliant and effective reality of how technology has moved. According to scidev.net, smaller countries such as Belize and Rwanda have seen great success in implementing

---

34   See Sci Dev Net, *Texting saves lives of HIV patients*, study confirms. Accessed at www. scidev.net/global/health/news/texting-saves-lives-of-hiv-patients-study-confirms.html

robust systems to track inventories on rolling out anti-retroviral treatment programmes.

In my radio show with Victor, I've had the pleasure of interviewing several entrepreneurs in this space. All of the following examples begin to unpack the amazing space digital payment services can play (and is beginning to play) in truly changing lives. It also showcases the business opportunities: According to the GSMA mHealth report, the global mHealth market is looking to exceed $30 billion (US).

VULA APP

Cataract surgery has become something rather commonplace and relatively routine in the West. It can literally take 20 minutes of treatment without major surgery. But in rural Africa it's a very different story.

Think about what it must be like to stay in a faraway village. It's not only difficult to get diagnosed —the nearest clinic or specialist could be hundreds of kilometres away, and transport is not cheap — but it's even more difficult for anything to be done about it even after diagnosis, leaving whole families without hope for something that could be resolved if they only had the right information and resources available to them.

In this case we look at South Africa, which arguably has plenty of facilities for cataract surgery in its major cities. About 1,300 kilometres from Cape town is the village of Kotyana, and for 72-year old Ndawayipheli and his wife Nojongile (68) it's not easy to just jump on a bus and travel to the city, receive a diagnosis, and then go back sometime later for the operation. The entire process is, quite frankly, unreachable for them.

I discovered the story of this couple at an article at the BBC.[35] Here is this beautiful village set amidst one of the most beautiful places in the country, but they can never enjoy it because they are blind from cataracts. While cataract surgery is offered at the nearby town of Mthatha, that's a four hour drive. Plus there is the small problem of a year-long waiting list.

Dr William Mapham, however, was not one to be set back with such challenges. Instead he looked at his smart phone and saw an opportunity, developing the Vula app (meaning "open" in Siswati, Xhosa and Zulu). It's a brilliant solution that makes use of what every smartphone has —a camera and data. Even in remote villages like Kotyana, data is available. Mapham, being a doctor, realised how difficult it is for people to get to him so he could see and diagnose them, which led him to this thought: what if he could get to them? But how? He couldn't be in two places at once.

Well, mobile technology changes that story. Through the app, health care workers do a vision test on the screen, which asks them a few questions, and after that's done the app takes a photograph of their eye. They then go through a checklist of common symptoms. The app uploads all of this to a database which specialists all over the country have access to. Amazingly, cataracts are easy to spot using photos (in fact, it's often better with a photo). The specialists then can diagnose the problem and recommend treatment, even going so far as booking an appointment at a specialist centre on behalf of the user. This resolves the lengthy process of having to get to a doctor for a diagnosis, put a name on the waiting list, and then go back for surgery —an expensive and lengthy process for people in remote villages.

---

35   See the BBC, *'My life is so much better now'.* Accessible at <u>www.bbc.com/news/health-31877594</u>.

Ndawayipheli's surgery changed her life. She told the BBC: "After the operation, my eye was covered for two days. On the third day I removed the patch and I could see! My life is so much better now. It was really bad when I was blind, I was even afraid to do a simple thing such as walking. I was afraid of hurting myself because I couldn't see where I was going."

Without the streamlining of this process that the Vula app brings, Ndawayipheli would probably still be blind today. That's the value and power of what technology is starting to do in our days.

This not only helps patients but doctors as well. See, doctors in rural areas are usually general practitioners and are under-qualified to treat problems such as cataracts. Only a specialist really knows what to look for or what to do about it. But the Vula app gives general practitioners a direct, easy, and accessible line to eye specialists and a system that works. Imagine how difficult it would be for a doctor to phone a specialist from a rural village asking for advice? With the Vula app, the doctor can also just take a picture of the eye and get it sent to the specialist, and help to book the necessary surgery and manage the process for their patient, learning as they go along.

Dr Amy Linde, one such doctor, told the BBC: "[the Vula app] allows us to access an experience level and level of knowledge that we may not have ourselves, or... things that we haven't seen before."

In other words, she is gaining new on-the-job experience and increasing her theoretical knowledge through the app!

Technology like the Vula app is making it much easier for doctors or even users to diagnose other common diseases in such areas, such as malaria and tuberculosis. The Vula app shows us that the specialist doesn't even need to be in the same village! It's no wonder that the Vula app won the MTN Innovative App of the Year, 2015!

THE GIFTEDMOM APP

When it comes to pregnancy, rural communities are usually at a loss. It's not just the factor of money —it costs to have scans and see a doctor once a month (if even that!) —but also a factor of time. The village might have a midwife, but they don't have all the right instruments and they don't have the know-how or information when something goes wrong. And unfortunately so many things can and do go wrong, resulting in high maternal mortality rates in such areas —most of which could have been avoided. The risk of dying in childbirth is actually very low in the developed world — one in 3,700 -—but this jumps to one in 38 in Sub-Saharan Africa.

Cameroon is on the very high mortality scale —one of the highest in the world —reporting 590 maternal deaths per 100,000 live births. About 64 percent of mothers in Cameroon receive no medical check-ups after their baby is delivered.[36] It seems that the issue is often that women simply don't know what to look for, what to expect, and how to gauge whether their newborn is doing well or not.

Alain Nteff, a 23 year-old Cameroonian, was quick to see how mobile technology could help with this problem. He saw that the mobile phone could put you in touch with anyone in the world —so why not put you in touch with medical advice?

In 2012 Nteff, 20 years old and studying engineering, visited a friend in rural Cameroon who was practising at a hospital.

---

36   See the World Health Organisation (WHO), *Trends in Maternal Mortality: 1990 to 2013.* Accessed at apps.who.int/iris/bitstream/10665/112682/2/9789241507226_eng.pdf

What he saw changed him forever. He witnessed several moms and newborns die because there just wasn't proper, even ordinary antenatal care. It all could have been avoided without much trouble at all. The situations could have been predicted and managed without a problem, had there been decent enough care. So him and his friend, Conrad Tankou, put their heads and hearts together and decided that surely they could do something about this.

> "I'm passionate about using technology to solve problems in my community, and I just saw it as an opportunity to apply my engineering to solve one of the world's biggest and oldest problems," Nteff told CNN.[37]

So what did they come up with? An SMS service. Moms-to-be and new mothers simply have to text the word MOM to the right number and they will receive a call back. Via SMS they can also text a question and receive a reply from a qualified doctor! By subscribing through the first text of "MOM" they receive advice about what to expect in their pregnancy and what to do. "We realised that there was a need to create a low cost channel to educate women on when they should go for antenatal care and when they should take their babies for vaccination," Nteff says.

This channel they called GiftedMom, an SMS service that has also developed into an app. The service quickly grew to 2,100 subscribers by 2015. It works with the Mobile Alliance for Maternal Action, a USAID-backed movement that uses mobile technology to improve maternal health in the developing world. Tankou

---

37   See CNN, *Alain Nteff, the 23-year-old savior of Cameroon's mothers and babies*. Accessed at edition.cnn.com/2015/02/17/africa/gifted-mom-cameroon-alain-nteff/

leads the team of doctors who find answers to the queries that come in.

> "The SMS we sent to the first pregnant woman was special — she said that when she read it she felt so much joy, and she was telling me 'I feel now that somebody's got my back,'" says Nteff.

It is low-cost. That's important. The subscription fee costs less than one U.S. dollar. Messages that include alerts for vaccinations or when a newborn is due are all free. Furthermore, they are currently also developing a voice technology for the four traditional languages of Cameroon.

Nteff sees this problem as not a woman issue but as a humanitarian issue. He says that everybody should take it seriously. "We all have mothers, we all have sisters, and it's not just a problem for women or girls. Our mission is really to create a world of mothers who are gifted. A world that is free of maternal and infant death — a world of gifted moms," he says. Guess what? The Queen of England agrees — endorsing the GiftedMom App under the umbrella of the first Queen's Young Leaders Award.

THIS QR CODE TAKES YOU TO AN INFOGRAPHIC AT CNN THAT PROVIDES A GRAPHICAL BREAKDOWN ON MATERNAL CARE IN CAMEROON.

ACCESS.MOBILE IN UGANDA

The same sort of thing is happening in Uganda with the ClinicCommunicator, run by Kaakpema Yelpaala, originally born in the U.S. But in this case it's a little different. ClinicCommunicator makes use of Cloud technology —doctors and medical personnel use the app to upload patient information, which can then be accessed by other medical personnel. This is important as patients don't have the luxury of a regular doctor or specialist. Through the service doctors can schedule and send a reminder to the patient about an appointment, provide the right details about their medicine, and remind them to pick it up, or send a script.

This all improves communication between the patient and doctors. The paper-based administration that takes place in most countries throughout Africa is burdensome and difficult, often creating a bottleneck and difficulty with communication. This over-rides all that and creates something clean, friendly, and much more easier, administratively.

Typically a front desk administrator might try to call patients to remind them of their appointment. But that administrator also deals with patient intake and all the front desk duties, and it is a lot of work, says Yelpaala at howwemadeitinafrica.com. "So there are often times when people don't receive those phone calls, and if they don't receive them they are more likely to miss their appointments."[38]

After completing his masters at Yale, Yelpaala got involved in several public health projects in Africa. Obviously, he came face to face with this administrative problem and the huge challenges involved. But it was his time at the Clinton Health Access Initiative in 2004, where he mainly worked into East Africa,

---

38 See How We Made It In Africa, *Yale graduate on starting a clinic-to-patient communication service in Uganda*. Accessed at www.howwemadeitinafrica.com/yale-graduate-on-starting-a-clinic-to-patient-communication-service-in-uganda/

that he started noticing the massive influence and adoption of the mobile phone in Africa —and he began to think of how this could serve as a solution.

In 2011, his journey in this direction had begun to crystallize. He founded a company called Access.Mobile which develops digital health solutions. By 2013 he was piloting the ClinicCommunicator in Uganda, building trust in the market with free trial periods to both public and private practitioners. (It runs on a subscription model.)

"Uganda is actually a great starting place to kind-of incubate an idea and try to validate a product concept," he says. "And the market had a lot of key requirements. It wasn't crowded in terms of health technology. There was improving telecommunications infrastructure, and wireless network infrastructure was expanding rapidly so there was improving connectivity throughout the country. And Ugandan healthcare providers were starting to be more open to technology tools to help them run their clinics and hospitals. So it was basically the convergence of those factors."

Microsoft gave Access.Mobile an award in 2014, one of five companies to win it, which involved grant money. "But even more [importantly] it involved all kinds of other support such as building the capacity of the team, software development, business strategy and helping us find new partners," says Yelpaala.

With this they began to add more capabilities to the app, including SMS-based vouchers and better engagement with patients with a lower income. Then, in partnership with Dutch-based PharmAccess Foundation, Access.Mobile has begun to move into Kenya as well. PharmAccess's focus is to make healthcare more accessible for lower-income groups, making this a fantastic and brilliant partnership.

But what I find interesting, for our purposes in this book, is how Yelpaala sees digital payment services as key in all this. He speaks of how digital payment services are partnering, and how regulations have morphed and changed to accommodate this new technology, by highlighting the big challenge of mobile technology: scaling from country to country.

> "I believe that in African markets you can come up with solutions that solve problems in a pan-Africa or global way," he says. "Cross-country scaling is really not that straightforward. And while we are getting enquiries for ClinicCommunicator from all over Africa, and even from some other parts of the world, we have to be very thoughtful about how we expand... given the realities of [different countries]."

The solution? Digital payment services. Why? Because telecommunication companies are already expanding and scaling across countries, as well as digital payment tservices such as M-Pesa.

We'll get to that in a moment. For now, let's look at one more example.

SPROXIL

We now turn our eyes to Ghana. Ashifi Gogo[39] is an interesting individual. When I interviewed him on radio I thought he had ingenious foresight. I hadn't ever imagined innovation in the pharmaceutical industry — partly due to my limited knowledge. But what intrigued me was how he's trying to solve a serious humanitarian issue with simple technology.

---

39   Follow him on Twitter at twitter.com/ashifi

Counterfeit medicine is a multi-billion problem that costs people their lives. Fake anti-malarial and tuberculosis drugs are the culprits behind 700,000 reported annual deaths alone. Fake medicine is not always toxic, but the problem is it's just not effective, and therefore people continue to take their medicine but never beat their infection. This not only has repercussions on people's lives but also on the culture —if the medicine didn't cure my father, why would it cure me? Perhaps I should look for alternative means or just wait it out.

As businessinsider.com reports,[40] in 2015, fake teething medicine was responsible for the death of 84 children in Nigeria. It's heartbreaking. The proper medicine uses a harmless, sweet solution to help the kids take the medicine; but the fake medicine substituted this for a poisonous chemical —it had the same taste, so no one suspected anything.

This has to be dealt with. In emerging markets, such as those in Africa, there are limited resources to help curb this sort of problem, giving counterfeiters more space to move and do their business. But, interestingly enough, crowdsourcing through mobile suddenly presents a new opportunity to curb the problem. And it is highly effective. In 2009, Sproxil was formed to help consumers be the ones to combat the drug counterfeit problem —all done via one simple text message.

This is how it works. Pharmaceuticals who partner with Sproxil include a unique code on the packaging. You can't see the code straight-away but need to scratch on the panel that covers it, and underneath you will find it. You SMS this code (for free) to the Sproxil number and it comes back and tells you if it's genuine or not. You can also do the same through an app, the web, or a

---

40   See Business Insider, *5 startups have a brilliant plan to tackle the deadly multibillion-dollar fake drug scourge.* Accessed at www.businessinsider.com/startups-who-are-tackling-the-counterfeit-drug-problem-2015-8

voice call.In this TEDx Boston video, Gogo explains how it all works. Scan the QR code below to check it out.

SEE ASHIFI GOGO EXPLAIN SPROXIL'S TECHNOLOGY IN THIS TEDx BOSTON VIDEO.

This is Sproxil's award-winning Mobile Product Authentication (MPA) product, and one can see how it can suit other kinds of products as well. It continues to be successful in the pharmaceutical industry, but now also supports the beauty & personal care industry, fast-moving consumer goods (FMCG), electrical goods, oil & gas, and agribusiness. Sproxil also now operates in five countries across three continents — covering Africa, America, Asia, and the Middle-East.

Derek Kerton, principal analyst at the San Jose, California-based wireless consultancy firm the Kerton Group, explains:

"By using the Sproxil solution to verify the authenticity of drugs, those at the bottom of the pyramid can fight back at those that would take advantage of them, and assure themselves safer medicines and better health."

When BIOFEM Pharmaceuticals in Nigeria decided to use Sproxil's MPA solution, in less than three months its Glucophage product sales increased more than ten percent in Nigeria, and

BIOCHEM saw a return of investment of over 1000 percent. And how have customers responded? Well, they now ask for sachets with Sproxil authentication labels. Demand for the genuine product goes up while counterfeit drugs cannot compete.

According to Partnership for Safe Medicines' Vice President Bryan Liang, SMS is a wonderful example of how technology can be used to protect patients and thwart illicit drug channels. Recently Liang has recommended the technology to the FDA in the U.S. "It's also an excellent method by which to reach health-care providers and affected patients about drug recalls and counterfeit warnings," Liang says. So we can see that an African solution is bringing solutions to the Western world.

And we start to see a link between digital payment services and healthcare. As Gogo says: "The increasing popularity of enhancing global health activities with private sector entrepreneurship signifies a shift in thinking among experts and practitioners. By wrapping our business model around providing purchase decision support to those with little, we believe they will save money and increase their well-being, bringing new, locally-driven momentum to achieving the MDGs."[41]

The most fascinating part for me with the Sproxil product revolves around law enforcement. What Sproxil is able to do, based on the Global Positioning System (GPS) location from which the SMS is sent, is map out hot spots where counterfeit responses to SMS's are frequently received from. What this means is that law enforcement agencies can use this in a targeted approach to combating counterfeit drug rings, where they've been going in blind in the past or receiving anonymous tips etc.

---

41   See Business Call to Action, *Pfizer, Vodafone, Sproxil and WaterHealth International Commit to Fight Poverty and Improve Health Care.* Accessed at www.businesscalltoaction. org/news-highlights/2010/09/pfizer-vodafone-sproxil-and-waterhealth-international-commit-to-fight-poverty-and-improve-health-care/

See the win-win? The poor have access to more information, the right medicine, and even doctors. Pharmaceutical companies are able to grow in the developing world as counterfeit medicine is dealt with. Law enforcement agencies get a more targeted approach. Entrepreneurs can provide the necessary creativity, business models, and resources to put everyone together.

LISTEN TO OUR RADIO INTERVIEW WITH ASHIFI GOGO FROM SPROXIL.

THE DIGITAL PAYMENT SERVICES LINK

Julienne Lauler from Mondato, a consulting firm in the digital payment services space, notes how digital payment services can provide a solution to the limitations of mHealth on its own. "Introducing mobile financial services within these platforms may offer a way to drive reduced costs and enhanced efficiency — resulting in more affordable, inclusive healthcare systems," she says.[42] Patricia Mechael, executive director of the mHealth Alliance, says that the inability of mHealth to scale-up is often due to a lack of alignment with national health priorities, as well as a lack of clarity within several areas, including the responsibility for financing, standards and policies that protect patient privacy, and, of course, technology.

Reliable financial systems to pay for the systems is one of the

---

42   See Mondato, MFS: TRANSFORMING HEALTHCARE IN EMERGING MARKETS. Accessed at mondato.com/blog/mfs-transforming-healthcare-in-emerging-markets/

other challenges for mHealth. Many developing nations only devote just five percent of their GDP to health, while others devote up to ten percent (Organisation for Economic Co-Operation and Development (OECD) countries). In such nations there is always underfunding, while staff and administration and systems are overburdened, resulting in broken supply chains, untrained workers and general inequality, a lack of access to information and transportation.

Digital payment services, however, can help to make business models more sustainable, raising the quality of healthcare and access. This also according to Menekse Gencer, mPay Connect founder, a consulting firm for mobile payments. Gencer is the lead author for the mHealth Alliance Report[43] which lists many of the benefits digital payments services can bring to this sector. Security, the paying of salaries, financial inclusion, the challenges of the poor, are all part and parcel of what is listed.

The Health Finance and Governance (HFG) Project —a five-year (2012-2017) project funded by the U.S. Agency for International Development, with the specific focus of improving health and finance and health governance systems in partner countries, also sees the benefit of digital payment services in this sector. "HFG… works with country partners to improve the management of health systems and generate much-needed evidence on the most effective, efficient ways to improve health systems," says the organisation.[44]

As per its website: "Mobile money systems have the potential to extend the reach of financial services to populations not served by the traditional banking sector. In sub-Saharan

---

43   Available at mhealthknowledge.org/images/content/publications/amplifying_impact.pdf
44   See www.hfgproject.org/about-hfg/project-information/

Africa, for example, 12 percent of the population without a formal bank account uses mobile phones to conduct financial transactions, and in at least 28 countries around the world, there are more mobile money agent outlets than formal bank branches."[45]

Part of the HFG's focus, therefore, is to promote the use of mobile phone-based payment solutions, which it believes expands priority health services to vulnerable populations. Digital payment services allow for people to much more easily get the funds for treatment through saving and insurance programs. In the following chapter we will look at insurance more closely, but here we begin to see an interesting link. As part of data and voice packages, telecommunications companies are adding in digital payment services, such as insurance. And one of those can be health insurance.

Digital payment services also allow for faster payments to doctors and healthcare providers, which has its own, very obvious, advantages, allowing for providers to increase their delivery and services. Moreso, this allows for secure transfers which reduces cash management costs (for both the patient and the provider), reduces logistical problems associated with cash, and the seamless transfers through digital payment services also reduces much of the administrative burdens and paperwork involved. As we've also seen, m-Health reduces the general administrative and paperwork issues that arise particularly in Africa.

But even more, digital payment services brings in security to both parties —it facilitates accountability and increases actual physical security, since patients and providers don't need to carry around cash. In a previous chapter we've highlighted the massive

---

45   See www.hfgproject.org/mobile-money-expands-financial-access-to-health-services/.

security benefits of digital payments services, and this plays a big part in this industry. Digital payments services also provide audit trails, which helps to improve efficiency and governance in this sector.

It even provides brilliant security to healthcare providers in the sector, in terms of the fact that salaries can get paid through it and it can facilitate pay-for-performance schemes, and so on. The latter is an interesting development. In Pakistan, the non-profit Indus Hospital (which calls itself 'Pakistan's first paperless hospital') uses digital payments services to financially reward health workers who screened for tuberculosis (TB) in their respective communities. The incentive helped for there to be a huge increase in reported TB cases (in fact, it more than doubled during the six months of this campaign). Digital payment services is therefore a tool which improves healthcare workers' performance, having a very positive knock-on effect.

Digital payments services also help the healthcare industry reach more people than it can in traditional ways. Imagine if healthcare providers could have access to digital payment services subscriber details? According to GSMA, citing an mHealth Alliance report, "mHealth providers can leverage [digital payment services] agent networks to accomplish shared or redundant tasks, such as signing up users, checking ID and registering phone numbers."[46] I can see the use of apps and cloud technology to help track subscriber's health. Telecommunication companies can get involved in all this as well. Some are even researching how mobile phones and digital payments services

---

46   See GSMA, *Mobile Money: Transforming Healthcare in Emerging Markets*. Accessed at www.gsma.com/mobilefordevelopment/programme/mhealth/mobile-money-transform-ing-healthcare-in-emerging-markets/

can help curb sexual violence.[47] The integration of these industries and approaches allows for each to grow, and as the mHealth
sector sees itself more financially stable through the use of digital
payment solutions, for-profit companies will see the value in
offering more health-focused products and services, and so it
continues to grow.

See how it all relates? Overall we see a system that promotes
financial inclusion, addresses the many financial barriers for the
poor (even the barrier of needing to draw cash), reduces risks on
numerous fronts, brings solutions to better governance, lowers
administrative burdens, and can deal with travel problems, and
opens up new health solutions to groups of people who would
otherwise never have access to these solutions, in addition to
creating some clever business opportunities. It's no wonder that
an entity like HFG is making a concerted effort to help its partnering countries transition to digital payment services solutions,
providing technical support, developing strategies, sharing information and best practices, identifying resources and partners,
and so on.

CHALLENGES

New technology always comes with resistance, even if the benefits
of the technology over old technology are obvious. It's also not
easy integrating new systems into established ones. Plus there are
privacy and security issues, particularly when it comes to medical
records. According to Vodafone's mHealth report, there needs to
be more research in how technology can improve health —governments in particular want to see this sort of research.

You can't change a government's age-old paper system to an

---

47   See Sci Dev Net, *Focus on Gender: role for mHealth in sexual violence.* Accessed at www.
scidev.net/global/icts/analysis-blog/focus-on-gender-a-role-for-mhealth-in-sexual-violence.
html

electronic one overnight! There is also training required and so on. Plus there are set-up costs and there is the issue, which we've highlighted, of the fragmented digital payments services industry —it's not easy to scale from country to country, and digital payment players are creating 'closed-loop' systems that can't always speak to each other.

The lack of research, however, is perhaps the biggest challenge right now. In 2013, two reviews addressed this problem, noting that most mHealth trial results were coming from rich countries, which may not apply in the poorer countries.

"For example, just three out 75 trials that aimed to assess whether mobile technology interventions for healthcare consumers could change health behaviour or improve disease management were conducted in developing countries. And none of the 42 trials of interventions designed to support communication among healthcare providers or between health services and patients were done in the developing world," says scidev.net.[48]

The reviews also noted that sometimes there was a misdiagnosis in photo-based apps, and "text message-based appointment reminders were better than no reminders, but were no better than reminders sent by traditional routes such as telephone or mail."

Caroline Free, a senior lecturer in epidemiology, led the reviews (published in PLoS Medicine in January, 2013). She was not being negative about the solutions, however. When it came to medicine there were positive results.

---

48   See Sci Dev Net, *Evidence Lacking on mHealth effectiveness in poor countries.* Accessed at www.scidev.net/global/health/news/evidence-lacking-on-mhealth-effectiveness-in-poor-countries.html

"Our systematic review shows there is good evidence that text messaging interventions can increase adherence to anti-retroviral medication and can increase smoking cessation," she says. "The effects of mobile phone based interventions appear promising in some other areas, but further high quality trials are required to establish their effects."

Her call is for there to be more research, and so there should be. On the other hand, Amanda Glassman of the Center for Global Development, writing earlier, notes that the global health community, for its part, has come to appreciate mHealth. What's needed, on her estimation, is co-ordination. "Coordination between funders and implementers is essential if the potential of mHealth is to be realised, she says.[49] In a summary of her comments at scidev.net, it notes:

"Coordination will help avoid the need for several mobile phones to access different mobile applications from different funding sources, or help systems such as the HIV/AIDS Health Management Information System of the President's Emergency Plan for AIDS Relief to reach beyond their initial application."

There needs to be alignment on standards and systems, ICT strategies that take note of the context, and information must be shared between all parties. Furthermore, Glassman argues that there must be a coalition of global health funders to improve co-ordination.

---

49 See Center for Global Development, *The Elusive Power of mHealth*. Accessed at www.cgdev. org/blog/elusive-power-mhealth

"If funders don't take deliberate steps now to measure outcomes, prioritise investments, and coordinate activities, there is a risk that the current hype will quickly fade and dollars will be directed towards the next big thing," she says.

In my opinion, digital payments services create a funding channel that can do all this. What we need are more Ashifi Gogo's, Alain Nteff's, Kaakpema Yelpaala's, and William Mapham's who are willing to stir their entrepreneurial creativity and keep their hearts engaged with the people and the needs of the community. We are sitting on the precipice of a very good future here.

"Originality is the essence of true scholarship.
Creativity is the soul of the true scholar."
—Nnamdi Azikwe, Nigerian Head of State, 1963 to 1966.

CHAPTER SEVEN

DISRUPTING EDUCATION

What kind of innovation could solve the education problem? Education has always been one of the biggest causes of the gulf between the developed and developing worlds.

Distance learning is not a new concept, but technology and the Internet have made it much easier and, in some cases, cheaper. Over the last few decades the concept of eLearning —electronic learning —has shown tremendous promise, and has certainly made for more opportunity in education. There has been easier access to quality education from many areas in the world where there was none, which has helped to empower individuals and even improve health (as we explored in our chapter on m-Health). But often projects to get children laptops and equip schools with computers and technology have not produced as much fruit as hoped.

There are several reasons for this. One is that technology simply evolves too quickly, and it doesn't always come cheap. By the time a government has rolled out its one-laptop-per-child programme, those laptops are already dated. Generally a laptop is not going to last much longer than five years, and even the cheapest models aren't really cheap —meaning, that if they break, there is also a huge cost in replacing, etc.

M-Learning (mobile learning) is the natural evolution of e-Learning, however. Defined as "learning across multiple contexts, through social and content interactions, using personal electronic devices," (according to Wikipedia), it allows students to learn virtually anywhere a mobile signal is available. This includes the use of mp3 players, laptops, and, of course, mobile phones and tablets, with the latter two becoming the most convenient and opening up unique opportunities.

Things drastically change when education moves to a mobile phone, especially given the penetration of mobile phones throughout Africa. The classroom is transcended. But it's important to remember that this doesn't mean the classroom is replaced. The question of whether face-to-face interactions in education are dispensable with new technology has been answered with an emphatic "no" by experts, such as the panel who sat at the Africa — Continent of Opportunities: Bridging the Digital Divide event in May 2015 in Berlin.

"While everyone recognised the benefits of e-learning — such as enabling distance education, asynchronous and synchronous communication in peer learning networks, and the ability to scale learning beyond fixed time and space constraints — they equally valued face-to-face-based education. Overall, the concept of complementarity, where both approaches are used in the most appropriate way, was seen as the ideal education model," says Steve Vosloo, an expert in the subject, summarising the discussion.[50]

A lot of M-learning is, to be sure, informal, but institutions can make use of it to greatly enhance education and fill in the gaps where they fall short. Even private schools like St Johns in Johannesburg encourage maths students in its primary school to hop on board an app called Mathletics which puts them into an online social network where they can compete in friendly geeky maths challenges against others from all over the world.[51]

The convenience of M-Learning, which is self-evident, is accessibility. With a smart phone and data you can access it from anywhere. As Wikipedia says: "Sharing is almost instantaneous among everyone using the same content, which leads to the reception of instant feedback and tips." Exam scores have been shown to increase twenty percent, with the drop-out rate in technical fields cutting 22 percent. Learning content can be tailored to the student and are much more interactive than simple textbooks.

The potential of m-Learning on mobile phones is fantastic when you look at the mobile penetration numbers. For example, a 2014 study in South Africa showed that while 22 percent of students had access to computers (this doesn't mean they owned one), 48 percent owned their own mobile phone, while 100 percent could have access to one. In Nigeria there are also positive numbers like these —five percent of the population have access to a computer, while 63 percent have access to mobile phones, meaning mobile phones are primary way through which people access the Internet.[52]

---

50   See Steve Vosloo, *e-Learning: "e" is for exchange, not electronic.* Accessed at stevevosloo. com/2015/05/18/e-learning-e-is-for-exchange-not-electronic/

51   See www.mathletics.co.za/

52   See Sovtech, *Mobile Rich & Education Poor — Is m-learning a solution for education in Africa?* Accessed at sovtech.co.za/mobile-rich-education-poor-is-m-learning-a-solution-for-education-in-africa/

Much of the innovation in m-Learning is coming from Africa itself. Rebecca Stromeyer, founder of the annual eLearning Africa conference, notes that "homegrown innovation and entrepreneurship have driven a boom in the sector".

> As journalist Guy Pfeffermann also notes, m-Education "has not caught on in high-income countries, where nearly everyone has access to computers and broadband. In sharp contrast, in Africa, mobile learning is the only practical way to sidestep huge physical and computing infrastructure deficits, and so allow busy people to learn wherever they happen to be at incredibly low cost. Mobile learning solutions have the potential to combine scalability, very broad geographical availability, very low unit costs, and the flexibility required to adapt to life in Africa."

This goes back to my previous chapter on how the lack of traditional infrastructure in Africa is leading to innovation and a new kind of infrastructure emerging. It's very exciting when you think about Africa becoming a technological leader in many respects. Pfeffermann's way of putting this point is quite nice: "In the case of business education, this may soon lead, counter-intuitively, to Africa becoming a global leader in mobile technological innovation."

UNESCO is one organisation which sees massive opportunities for mobile learning in Africa, and is implementing solutions into higher education, where many believe it can fit most naturally. As it says in its report, Turning on Mobile Learning in Africa and the Middle East,[53] "Mobile learning also enables an

---

53   *Turning on Mobile Learning in Africa and the Middle East,* 2012. Accessed at unesdoc. unesco.org/images/0021/002163/216359e.pdf

improvement in the quality of education by opening up new avenues for informal, personalised and situated learning. In addition, mobile learning can potentially promote social equity by allowing marginalised groups access to decision-making. This evolving value proposition offers an opportunity to leverage the ubiquity of mobile phones in addressing the systemic crisis in education in the region."

This isn't all just about governments and education departments and NGOs, though, as we shall see. There is a huge opportunity waiting for the private sector in this space. Here again, I believe, digital payments services can not only play a part in bringing in profits but also in truly changing people's lives. McKinsey has categorically stated that "by 2020, mEducation could be a USD 38 billion revenue opportunity for mobile operators."[54]

But how? Let's go through some of the ways that mobile technology is changing the education environment and then discuss exactly how digital payments services can enhance this technology and create more opportunity for people of lower income groups to access education.

BYE TO BOREDOM

Remember how boring your textbook at school was? Remember your parents complaining about how expensive it was? Remember trying to stuff it in your bag and find space for it? Mobile devices take away all these negatives as textbooks become interactive with video, touch screen, and other visual aids. Also, downloading a textbook is theoretically cheaper than buying one (the costs involved in printing are circumvented). This has made the

---

54   See McKinsey & Company, *Transforming learning through mEducation.* Accessed at mckinseyonsociety.com/transforming-learning-through-meducation/

textbook an interactive experience and tool, rather than just a reference book.

Wi-Fi and data allow for information to be accessed instantly. This also has advantages to the actual updating of information. Your textbook, in the old days, could often be out of date with the latest finds in the given study. Now information can be updated instantly on the Internet and the app used on the mobile phone updated as well, with a single touch.

It's been shown that mobile devices can enhance group collaboration with the students, given the communication options and the interactivity of the devices. Students become part of online communities for learning. The Mathletics app, mentioned earlier, serves as an example.

Parents and students and teachers are able to collaborate through the use of mobile technology. Parents can be updated more regularly as to progress. Students can interact with each other through apps and platforms. Teachers can be involved in the process from end to end. Learning takes place, therefore, not only inside but also outside the classroom.[55]

From SMS to more modern forms of mobile communication, distance education has been (and can further be) greatly enhanced. This is also great for students who have to be mobile and people in business who are receiving training and cannot afford to actually be away from their job.

Interestingly, podcasting has shown to be a major tool for learning. Students don't need to actually go to lectures, and they can record and play back themselves to rehearse their own oral presentations. Podcasting can also be used to great effect in providing additional learning on a certain subject. In research published in 2009 by Callaway & Ewan, it was shown that uni-

55   For more see FutureLab, *Literature Review in Mobile Technologies and Learning.*

versity students who downloaded podcasts of lectures managed to achieve much higher results in exams than those who actually attended in person. This is a very interesting development. It doesn't mean that in-person lecturing should be disposed of, but rather that m-Learning can supplement the process considerably. Webinars, as another example, which can be done on simple applications such as Google Hangouts, allow for learning over distance with a lecturer to become quite interactive. Already there are online education opportunities where you can attend language classes and more, using a webinar interface. Here you can view a live lecture and ask questions in a live environment, and still access the lecture later.

AT WORK

The workplace actually benefits considerably from all these developments, with training happening on-the-job in a much more seamless way. More employees can be reached much more effectively with mobile learning, without needing to take them all away for a week and train and then, later, have to re-train on the job.

CHALLENGES

There are challenges to mobile learning, mainly in the device itself — for example, battery life, actual connectivity, the screen size, software and standards (Apple, Android, Windows), and even a blending of the work / life balance that isn't very healthy. There is also the digital divide, but Africa seems to be quite able to manage this, given the penetration of cellphones in the market. There is a need for support though.

The growth of offline options, however, is certainly helping to curb data challenges. And as things develop there are holes being filled in with regards to software and standards. So there is tremendous promise here, as outlined by the study Mobile Enhanced Learning in a South African Context:[56]

> "Although e-learning has been revolutionary in educating a widely dispersed global population, Africa must consider its unique adoption of mobile technology and take the necessary steps to fill the educational void. There is no doubt that the effectiveness of m-learning will encounter heated debate, however if we are to consider the alternatives, global trends and current available information, it seems m-Learning is an industry to keep an eye on as Africa seeks a solution to its educational woes."

With this all in mind, let's look at some examples of African companies which are experimenting and finding success in this space.

FUSION MOBILE

In 2012, Dr Odum Ikechukwu formed Fusion Mobile Nigeria Limited, for the purpose of providing "world-class education for Africa with a primary focus on Nigeria." This was in response to the need he saw after teaching some students preparing for West African Examination Council (WAEC) Exams and Joint Admission Matriculation Board Exams (JAMB). During his research on ways to help these students, who seemed to know far less than they could, he stumbled upon Khan Academy[57], a nonprofit formed by Salman Khan which produces short, free lectures in a YouTube format and also makes use of an Internet-based dashboard (registration required). He realised that if he tweaked Khan's method he could find a way to solve the problem he was

---

56   *Mobile Enhanced Learning in a South African Context* (2013) by Mmaki Jantjies and Mike Joy. Accessed at www.ifets.info/journals/18_1/25.pdf

57   See www.khanacademy.org/

encountering. The main tweak had to do with video streaming, given how much data is required to do this. So he began to think of an app on the mobile phone which could solve this problem, provide the right kind of value, and function offline.

His app, Fusion Mobile, launched in 2014, includes a personalised learning dashboard, educational resources, 2,000 micro-lectures in video, and over 100,000 exercises and quizzes in the fields of mathematics, finance, biology, physics, chemistry, art history, economics, music, computer science, government, and English. These can be made available offline and anyone can access it and use the resources available. The mission of Fusion Mobile is to bring a "quality e-learning experience on the go to every Nigerian Student at the comfort of their phones, tablets and computers, [striving] to fill the need for quality education in a virtual learning environment."

According to Fusion Mobile, the ability for the student to interact with the app —to be able to fast forward or rewind a lecture —empowers them in unique ways.

"The power of this approach is that the student no longer sees teaching and learning as one boring classroom exercise, but an exciting educational game which absolute control he has. Our thinking is simple: students love to play with their mobile gadgets, why don't we make them have the classrooms in those gadgets and come out with flying colours?"

After learning through a lecture, the student is able to access a database of practical exercises, such as quizzes. There is also an exam mode which the student can turn on and practice exam questions. The answers are marked and graded immediately by the app, and the student is given valuable info in terms of where they have done well and where they haven't. This practice not only helps them in that respect but also gives them the necessary practice in writing an exam itself.

But one of Fusion Mobile's challenges is funding. The organisation, therefore, relies on donations and support from associations and individuals. It also costs $50. But what if there was another way to fund it? I think there just may be, if we think in the realm of digital payments services. I'll expand on that as we go along.

EFIKO AND GIDIMO

Efiko (www.efiko.com.ng), which started in 2012, is yet another example. It is an "interactive social testing and learning platform that enables learners to take curriculum-based tutorials and tests on their mobile devices." In its beginning days it was tested to great effect in eight schools, and has shown tremendous promise. It includes a leader board where students are encouraged to rank better, and it has the ability for students to challenge other students on social media with quizzes. Students can also see where other students go to school with a map, encouraging a social life.

Gidimo, also from Nigeria, is another example of this kind of learning. As per its website: "With a large proportion of the 400m Africans below the age of 25 living in environments with severely deficient educational infrastructure, Gidimo was born of a desire to help young Africans to learn, grow, and BE all that they can BE." It contains 70,000 preparation and test questions with learning material geared for young Africans' personal and professional lives. It's not just about learning information but also about helping with life skills. Furthermore, the app offers a chat facility and social network integration —users can share images, read the news, or even check flight and movie schedules, look up live scores for major worldwide sports, and get lifestyle tips. The idea is to create an online hub for young people where they get everything you would get from a university —not just the lectures and the learning, but the social life as well.

It also functions as a platform for other apps, in addition to offering corporate solutions, selling the platform to companies who can use it for on-the-job training and education. Furthermore, it is able to fund itself via selling examination scenario preps, job tests and professional course practices.

The platform, interestingly enough, sees the value of gamification in learning. Gamification is a relatively new term, so if you're unfamiliar with it, let me explain. It is when a learning experience or a working environment is built to function as a game (a quiz is a very basic example of this kind of learning). In partnership with Diamond Bank, Gidimo's Diamond Bank National Prep Challenge is a gamified approach to helping improve the high failure rates in national senior school leaving exams. Students are awarded with airtime vouchers when they score a certain amount of points.

If you're reading between the lines, you can begin to see some ways in which mobile learning can be funded —through corporate sponsorship, through the selling of certain material, and through the selling of games. But out of all these I find the idea of giving students airtime vouchers the most interesting. Why? Because it starts speaking into the realm of digital payment services. Can digital payments solutions find a way to bring education to people and fund it, at the same time?

BRCK'S KIO KIT

In chapter 3 I introduced you to BRCK (pronounced BRICK), which is based out of Kenya and has partners in the U.S. The

BRCK is a portable Wi-Fi hotspot and battery extender. When the power goes out, it kicks in and keeps you connected and able to work for many more hours. One of the biggest challenges with technology in the classroom is battery life for devices. Most devices when used at their maximum will only last for a couple of hours — whereas a normal school day is about eight hours. Aside from the charging of the devices being disruptive to the intent around mEducation, it moves the teacher from being, well a teacher, to IT support. You can probably appreciate that most teachers aren't equipped to be this, or didn't sign up for that!

Also, conditions such as inconsistent electricity supply can make this task quite a challenge. If the supporting services to these mEducation implementations aren't implemented correctly, one can imagine teachers abandoning these technologies and reverting back to the traditional pen and paper approach.

This is where BRCK saw a massive opportunity. Its devices already included a USB port and micro web server, which the company realised had many uses. Knowing the educational challenges highlighted here, BRCK developed the Kio, a toughened-up tablet at low cost that provides a very long battery life, easy to use interface, durability, and flexibility.

But the question is, how did they keep the cost low to make it suit an education budget? They built it by combining the BRCK with the Raspberry Pi. You might be familiar with the Raspberry Pi. It's a low-cost, credit-sized computer that can plug into any computer monitor or TV or touchscreen, and can use any standard mouse or keyboard. It runs on very basic software and you can easily learn to program it to your needs (using Python and Scratch languages). A Raspberry Pi 2 complete starter kit (which comes with a case and MicroSD and a whole lot of other goodies) costs in the region of $60. A Raspberry Pi computer on its own costs about $30. It can be programmed to do just about anything.

The Kio is basically a BRCK which enables access to locally-cached and web-hosted content. As stated by the company: "This was in line with our ethos of promoting equality in education and levelling the playing field by using the same technologies as the rest of the world but tweaked to our particular context."

But even though the Kio provides significant battery life, BRCK realised that charging it would still pose a challenge, and tablets can also easily go missing. Its solution was the Kio Kit — truly forward thinking. The Kio Kit is basically a suitcase which can be locked and can store up to forty Kio tablets at the same time —and here's the revolutionary part: they charge wirelessly.

Speaking to one of the co-Founders, Philip Walton, on my radio innovation segment, it was clear as day that there was a personal confluence between his entrepreneurial spirit, passion for technology, and love for children and education. Once again, it's an example of entrepreneurs finding ways to build new infrastructure in Africa where there typically has been none.

AFRICAN LEADERSHIP ACADEMY (ALA)

Most people who meet Fred Swaniker, co-founder of African Leadership Academy (ALA) and African Leadership University (ALU), are immediately impressed with his larger-than-life dreams for Africa. Two days after having Fred on my radio segment, ALU was named the third "Most Innovative Company of 2016 in Africa" by FastCompany. This is right behind M-Pesa and just before Samsung Electronics! To give a sense of the size of the problem Fred is addressing, the Huffington Post summarized it so well in an article written by Jenny J. Chen: "In 2013, 1.7 million students registered for Nigeria's college exams, all competing for the half million places available, which left over a million qualified college-age Nigerians without access to college education. And this is despite the fact that the number of universities in Nigeria has grown from 51 to 128 since 2005.[58]" This is a challenge all too prevalent across Africa, that there are simply so many qualified professionals but no opportunities. But Fred saw an opportunity and chose to reinvent the system.

ALA is a residential, secondary education campus just on the outskirts of Johannesburg in South Africa. It offers a two-year curriculum in Africa Studies and Entrepreneurial Leadership, in addition to the usual academic core studies. It's not just about the studies but also providing an environment for connecting and networking future leaders together. It seeks out and identifies leaders across Africa, based on a variety of factors, and chooses the most outstanding students to attend its two-year pre-University program. "The Academy was founded on the philosophy that a new generation of ethical, committed leaders is the key to Africa's development. ALA is the training ground for these future leaders," says the organisation. Solomon Martey, as an example, invented a borehole machine from spare parts that was able to pump, purify, and distribute water for his entire village. His invention was picked up by the Ghanaian Ministry of Environment and is being rolled out through many villages throughout the country. It's this kind of person that the ALA seeks to develop.

Every July and August, selected students from across the world attend its Global Scholars' Program. The idea is this: help them develop a powerful intellectual foundation, develop their lead-

---

58   See Huffington Post, *Innovators Changing Education, Health By Thinking Outside The Box*. Accessed at www.huffingtonpost.com/entry/innovators-changing-education-health-by-thinking-outside-the-box_us_56746bbee4b0b958f6569f23?ir=Technology&section=us_technology&utm_hp_ref=technology

ership capacity, encourage their entrepreneurial spirit through academic and practical hands-on programmes, and connect them together. It provides them unique opportunities to connect and experience the world outside of this as well: for example, Moroccan Iman Bermaki was given an opportunity to speak at the Mo Ibrahim Forum in Senegal, alongside former presidents.

Students' performance at ALA also sets them up for university bursaries, internship programmes, future employment, and so on. At the time of writing this book, 735 young leaders, representing 45 countries in Africa, have come through the programme. Their average age? 21. The stats and ventures and results of all this are so every encouraging.[59] This kind of approach to education really feels like the future to me. In many ways, Africa's education challenges are now starting to create new educational models that have the potential to shape how the future will look all around the world. From mEducation to reinventing the system altogether, there is a bright future here.

Fred is now extending the dream by rolling out 25 universities across Africa that would rival Ivy League schools across the globe. He has opened up two universities in Mauritius and Rwanda, and Nigeria is next.

LISTEN TO OUR INNOVATION INTERVIEW WITH
FRED SWANIKER FROM ALA.

---

59   For more, check out the website at www.africanleadershipacademy.org/our-impact/.

On the day of our radio interview, fifteen minutes before he was meant to come on air, he explained to me his vision for the university: combining traditional brick and mortar facilities with digital classrooms. All this felt futuristic to me until he pulled out virtual reality goggles, told me to put them on, and watch what a digital classroom would look like. It was probably the most revolutionary thought process I've come across in a very long time. Without a doubt, Fred has, is and will definitely be changing the education landscape in Africa. Re-imagining education!Listen to the radio segment interview with Fred Swaniker.

REVENUE OPPORTUNITIES

McKinsey's white paper, in partnership with GSMA, Transforming Learning through M-Education[60] opens up some thinking around the topic of funding these kinds of ventures, projecting that mEducation will become a USD 70 billion market by 2020 and that mobile operators stand to benefit from this in a huge way — saying it will become a "USD 38 billion revenue opportunity for mobile operators." Educational app downloads (free and paid) grew faster than the overall market, between 2009 —2011, says McKinsey. It also found that consumers are willing to spend more on educational apps than entertainment apps. At the time it noted several acquisitions in the market, such as Providence Equity Partners acquiring BlackBoard Inc. in 2011 for around USD 1.64 billion; the sale of a 90 percent stake in Wireless Generation to News Corporation in 2010 for approximately USD 360 million; and Research in Motion's acquisition of Chalk Media in 2008 in an all-cash deal of USD 18.7 million. These were pilot projects that became viable business models.

---

60   2009 — 2011: McKinsey White Paper on mEducation. Accessed at mckinseyonsociety. com/downloads/reports/Education/mEducation_whitepaper_April%201_vFINAL.pdf

For mobile operators, McKinsey sees an opportunity in what they do already —provide connectivity. "Under this strategic posture, MNOs [mobile operators] target the education segment with their range of connectivity products and services. The MNOs would provide learners, teachers and other education professionals with the scale and coverage to access educational content and solutions provided by other players in the education ecosystem. This would provide access to a global connectivity-linked revenue pool of USD 4 billion out of the total mEducation product opportunity of USD 38 billion in 2020."

And so here is where digital payment services come in. On the one hand, digital payment services can offer a unique way to help educational institutes. They provide a platform from which users can pay for school fees and so forth, but also provide a platform to bridge institutions with mEducation platforms that will enhance the institution's offering. If we apply this kind of thinking on the ground, by buying a data package with a particular service provider, for instance, you might get their digital payment service which gives you access to an educational app if you pay your school fees through the digital payment service. The idea is to target learners with special packages and offerings, and bring business to business activities to the education market. More than that, mobile operators can provide connectivity to schools and institutions — make Vodafone or MTN your service provider of choice and it will come and install a WiFi offering on campus, which the students can use to access mEducation apps and platforms from the campus. The added benefit, too, is the service provider can monitor and filter where the students are going —in other words, they also provide a safe Internet environment on campus, making parents even happier to go with that service provider.

As you can see, some clever out-of-the-box thinking allows for multiple services to come together, and those best poised to provide these are, in fact, mobile operators and those in the digital payment services space. McKinsey's white paper suggests that if mobile operators invest in the mEducation ecosystem, by building other capabilities adjacent to their connectivity options, it would unlock an even larger revenue pool.

> "Services that MNOs could build include secure cloud-based storage and hosting, data management and analytics, content management and delivery, and IT application hosting. Integrated operators with existing IT services capabilities are well-positioned to capitalise on the opportunity. MNOs could develop systems and interfaces to allow for secure user identification and billing of digital services provided by third parties. This would provide MNOs with a privileged position to support mEducation solutions such as e-books and games. For example, SingTel recently launched a platform called Skoob that allows customers to pay for e-books through their phone bills."

Then there are end-to-end services that include in-house content and devices. This, says McKinsey, could "throw open the entire mEducation opportunity of USD 70 billion". Two examples, Telefonica (Spain) and Korea Telecom (KT), have explored such options. It's true that McKinsey sees the biggest opportunity in mEducation to come from developed nations (North America, specifically) but given the massive need in Sub-Saharan Africa for such platforms, and the massive cellphone penetration in the continent already, and the successes we've already seen, I really do think there is a brilliant opportunity here.

IT'S NOT A SILVER BULLET

Only teachers can really ensure the success of mobile learning, and so they need to be given a more central role. ALA proves that this is so —with the right programme, and the right technology, and the right teachers, new things happen. This means that investors need to think of investing into current educational institutions and institutions such as ALA when they invest in this opportunity. Niall Winters from the Knowledge Lab of the University of London notes that only projects that work with education systems will improve learning and cut poverty. "We need to create an alternative vision that values and prioritises teacher involvement in mobile learning," he says.[61]

Bill and Melinda Gates have written that, "Better software will revolutionise learning," and I do agree with them. I don't want to sound as if I think mEducation and digital payment solutions are the silver bullet to solving all of Sub-Saharan Africa's educational challenges (and I don't think the Gates see it that way either), which is why ALA is something that excites me. I think all this working together is a step in the right direction. There is opportunity here that can be explored; and an opportunity that can truly change lives and, at the same time, make for good business.

---

61 See Sci Dev Net, How Teachers in Africa are failed by mobile learning. Accessed at www. scidev.net/global/education/opinion/how-teachers-in-africa-are-failed-by-mobile-learning.html

I am not an optimist, but a great believer of hope."
—**Nelson Mandela**

CHAPTER EIGHT

MICROINSURANCE: INNOVATION FINDS A SOLUTION

W e're all no strangers to risk, vulnerability and uncertainty. For the world's poorest, however, there is significantly more vulnerability. A natural disaster can cripple them for life. One season of crops failing is the end of all they have. With severe shifts in weather in recent years, thanks to climate change, and unreachable medical services, the world's poor live in a very dangerous world. When disaster strikes they do not have savings or insurance or investments to help bail them out. It's not just individuals but whole families who live in this space. Often they might have to rely on a loan, which comes at a high interest rate, because commercial banks see them as too much of a risk, and the informal sector most often is filled with loan sharks.

Governments haven't been able to alleviate the problem, either, for many reasons. It is often the informal economy that is in the direst need. Government's social protection schemes are often offered to its own formal sector employees, and for a government to take risks and make an investment may be asking too much.

This is the poverty cycle. There is a real vulnerability to disaster and when disaster happens, the result is even more poverty, making them increasingly vulnerable.

But as far back at the 1800's, a new idea emerged to help people out of this cycle: insurance. It first emerged as a mutual protection scheme among factory workers, meaning it was originally built for those with a low income. In those days, the wealthy didn't need insurance because they were in the very fortunate position of being able to self-insure. But as things progressed and insurance gradually became more sophisticated, and the wealthy and middle-class began to realise the value of insurance, this service offering has essentially become something only the wealthy and middle-class enjoy.

This little bit of history should immediately make us realise that there must be a way in which those of lower incomes can afford insurance. Business needs to rethink its strategy and product offerings. Most insurers have not designed products and delivery methods to suit the low income market —brokers, agents, and even direct sales are simply unable to do the job. Complex exclusions, legalese on contracts, complicated methods of claiming, and pricing are all turn-offs for the world's poor. Furthermore, the culture within insurance companies is usually one where salespeople are encouraged to hook in larger and more profitable clients.

Not to mention the fact that poorer people have a certain bias against insurance. The reality is that insurance is something you cannot see and hold in your hands, so paying an agreed amount to a company that provides you an unseen service unless you claim doesn't make sense. It is a risk for the poor to take out insurance —something actually might never go wrong, in which case the money seems wasted. Richard Leftley, CEO of UK-based MicroEnsure, says that turning up in towns and villages and asking poor families to buy insurance simply doesn't work.

> "Trying to explain to someone with no prior experience of insurance that if you pay even just a little bit every month then someone will pay you back if your crops failed or your child is hospitalised is often met with a perfectly understandable 'yeah right' response," he says.[62]

> In a short, five minute documentary on Micro-Insurance in East Africa, one business-savvy man tells his view: "Why should I invest my 10,000 insuring myself while I've got kids? I can invest this money somewhere else and at the end of the year, I would have made something out of that money." A small-business owner also admits that he lacks knowledge on these matters, while another business owner says, "I'd love to insure my business, but with my small capital I see no reason to insure."

SCAN THIS QR CODE TO WATCH UNDERSTANDING MICRO-INSURANCE IN EAST AFRICA, A SHORT FIVE MINUTE DOCUMENTARY.

And thus, in walks micro-insurance, which looks to solve these problems. An emerging industry since the early 2000's, micro-in-

---

62   See The Guardian, *Can microinsurance protect the poor?* Accessed at www.theguardian. com/global-development/poverty-matters/2011/feb/21/micro-insurance-protect-poor

surance helps to alleviate the vulnerability of poorer people and create a highly profitable insurance business. Coupled with digital payment solutions, micro-insurance is able to truly change lives.

HOW IT WORKS

Micro-insurance uses the mobile money service scheme to sell insurance policies en masse. A micro-insurance company has to balance coverage (how it reaches people, and who it will reach); cost (to the insurer); and affordability for the clients.

These goals can be reached by partnering with digital payment services. By using one of these services, customers are very often given incentives. As we've discussed previously, it's a case of "use our mobile money service, and receive free [insert product here]". One of these incentives is micro-insurance. The insurance can be built into a monthly fee for using the service, or a per-transaction fee. The insurance can also cover for just a week or a set time. Micro-insurance also generally protects individuals from very specific pitfalls —death, natural disasters, crop failures, or drought.

By being specific about the kind of insurance and being flexible on how long the insurance covers the individual for, the costs can be brought down. This also incentivises the poor to see the value in insurance. For example, if you are going to be travelling a longer distance than usual, you can use your mobile phone to buy some insurance for just that week. The ability to use your mobile money service and mobile phone helps to take away much of the complexity of insurance, and greatly increases how many people an insurer can reach.

Micro-insurance companies look to create very localised products, as this is key in reaching the right people. The Micro Insurance Academy (MIA), a not-for-profit which provides technical assistance to organisations looking at microinsurance, works with localised partners to help them design their own insurance packages specific to communities, understanding that the community will then see higher value in the product. "MIA does not sell or underwrite insurance. Instead, we provide local partners with the technical skills and guidance to operate and govern their own insurance schemes, because we believe the schemes will be more successful if the community has full ownership."[63] Bigger corporations have taken on the same principle, looking to find ways where a very localised sort of insurance can be offered. This helps for the poorer to see the benefit —it speaks to their context.

Speaking to the local context is proving to be one of the key strategies of business in Africa and in creating sustainability and addressing poverty. For example, Rwanda's cow donation project, Girinka ("May you own a cow") takes into account indigenous knowledge and practice by having the government work with select villages in taking care of a dairy cow. "Under the agreement, beneficiaries of Girinka pass on the first female offspring of the cow to a poor and malnourished neighbour approved by community leaders," says Chika Ezeanya at scidev.net.[64] Within six years of the project having begun, child malnutrition across the country dropped to 21 percent. The government could have adopted a more top-down approach, but it has realised that working with communities in their context makes more sense.

That is why partnerships with telecommunications and mobile financial services have been key in the micro-insurance idea. It speaks to the context and the culture of today's Africa. In fact, it has helped to revive micro-insurance in many ways,

---

63   See www.microinsuranceacademy.org/why-insurance/
64   See Sci Dev Net, A model for development built on indigenous foundations. Accessed at www.scidev.net/global/enterprise/opinion/development-indigenous-foundations.html

as micro-insurance corporations previously struggled with effective ways of how to deliver their product. MicroEnsure says that it now conducts most of its business in Africa by partnering with mobile phone companies and telecommunications. The incentive is often based on loyalty — if you are loyal to the provider you can receive insurance. If you buy a monthly prepaid card, you can get a month's insurance without having to pay extra. People find more value in paying for airtime than they do in paying for insurance, which is what makes this model so brilliant.

And, in truth, it is actually improving their lives. In fact, it is changing the lives of 500 million people today throughout the world![65] This option also helps to alleviate the problem that's come with micro-credit, where many poor families are simply unable to pay.[66] It's not a way of exploitation, either.

AN EXAMPLE MODEL

MicroEnsure has three different models. As per Leftley:

> "The first is a 'frequent user' model where the subscriber gets rewarded with higher levels of life insurance the more that they spend on airtime. So the more I spend in February the more free cover I get in March. The telco [telecommunications company] is willing to pay the premium as they profit from increased usage."

The second model, says Leftley, is tied to mobile payment platforms. "The subscriber chooses to buy insurance and pays small

---

65   See University of Stellenbosch Business School (USB), *Africa provides vast potential for micro-insurance.* Accessed at www.usb-ed.com/content/Pages/Africa-provides-vast-potential-for-micro-insurance.aspx

66   See The Guardian, *Impoverished Indian families caught in deadly spiral of microfinance debt.* Accessed at www.guardian.co.uk/world/2011/jan/31/india-microfinance-debt-struggle-suicide

premiums each month —the model here is that it is easier for a poor person to pay a small regular amount than to pay for insurance in one lump sum upfront.

The third model is tying insurance into a post-paid contract for the middle income market.

Part of the motivation is to get insurance out to millions of people who will begin to see the benefit. "Once people see that insurance works and that it pays out money, they will be willing to graduate to more expensive products such as health," says Leftley.

MicroEnsure's products include health policies, life insurance, disability insurance, redundancy insurance (losing your job), political violence insurance (an interesting addition that takes the local context in mind), property insurance, and weather index insurance —insurance against the effects of adverse weather risk. This last one is interesting as well, as it speaks directly into local agricultural challenges. Let's check it an example in Kenya.

KILIMO SALAMA

When the worst drought in 60 years hit the Horn of Africa in 2010, ten million people were badly affected with famine, with farmers' livelihoods set to go up in smoke. But fortunately, the microinsurance scheme "Kilimo Salama" in Kenya was able to offset the predicament. At the time it paid out US$3,135 each to more than 1,200 farmers for losses after lack of rain, and more than 1,400 farmers received US$9,230 each in September because of prolonged droughts that caused crop failure.

"The number of farmers willing to protect their crop by insuring their farm investments has increased tremendously. The sum insured among interested farmers has also been growing," said Wairimu Muthike at the time, the project's lead field coordinator.[67] Finance comes purely through the premiums collected from the farmers, and not through some charity scheme (which is often the case). Specific crop types were targeted, which helped farmers to see the value. "[Farmers] find this to be an effective way of ensuring that, when adverse effects of nature set in, they can find an alternative source of funding in order to cultivate again," said Silas Waweru, a farmer who benefited from the payout.

This is an example of how much this can help farmers. But it's interesting to note that many microinsurance schemes are coupled with charities. Does this mean it is unprofitable?

PROFITABILITY

Microinsurance can be unprofitable, but it doesn't have to be. Dr Ola Oyekan, research and development specialist at RGA Reinsurance Company of South Africa, who has conducted a study in South Africa and Nigeria, says micro-insurance products can be profitable for commercial insurance, with average profitability at 10 percent. Oyekan adds that better distribution channels are key, and mobile technologies are the forefront of such channels (retailers and funeral parlours are also popular, particularly in South Africa). "The mobile phone, in particular, has been identified as one of the best ways to distribute microinsurance products in emerging markets, with huge potential for cost savings," says RiskSA.[68]

"South Africa has one of the highest penetration rates of microinsurance policies worldwide, and this is largely through funeral policies," says Oyekan. "Global consultancy KPMG notes that only 15 per cent of South Africans have a short-term insurance policy, highlighting the need for insurance for lower income

---

67   See Sci Dev Net, *Micro-insurance scheme pays off for Kenyan farmers*. Accessed at www. scidev.net/global/farming/news/micro-insurance-scheme-pays-off-for-kenyan-farmers.html

68   Risk Africa Magazine. See www.risksa.com/micro-insurance-products-profitable-study/

groups and insurance more affordable while remaining profitable for companies."

Some newer numbers, expected to be released in 2016's Landscape of Microinsurance in Africa (Microinsurance Network), have much more to tell for the Sub-Saharan and Middle-East and North Africa regions. According to the preliminary briefing note, "Total written microinsurance premiums amounted to almost USD 647 million, representing an impressive 31% comparable increase since 2011... Interestingly, this growth was identified not just in credit life products but across all product lines."[69] Life covers dominate the region, but there has been tremendous growth in health and agricultural covers. The study shows that only 5.4 percent of the population in these regions are covered, totalling at 61.9 million people. South Africa now has the most coverage, with Ghana coming in second. Well, you can do the maths on the opportunity here![70]

LEGISLATION

Governments are getting on board, and we can see how micro-insurance is addressing their challenges. South Africa has legislation that has gone into effect from January 2016 which "aims to support financial inclusion in South Africa by means of providing a regulatory framework within which affordable insurance products can be sold to low income households in South Africa." The framework will intend to protect policy holders without placing an onerous regulatory or financial

---

69   See Micro Insurance Network, *The Landscape of Microinsurance in Africa 2015 —Preliminary Briefing Note.* Accessed at www.microinsurancenetwork.org/groups/landscape-microinsurance-africa-2015-preliminary-briefing-note

70   See more at www.microinsurancenetwork.org/sites/default/files/MIN-Africa%20Brief%20EN_A4.pdf.

burden on these companies.[71]

> There are informal providers of this kind of insurance, and these will now see regulation. As RiskSA notes, South Africa is "mulling the promulgation of micro insurance regulation to ensure that consumers are protected, with the understanding that if this sector is to flourish, current legislation governing insurers and intermediaries cannot be applied to the micro insurance industry. Legislation would encourage funeral parlours, cooperatives and other similar players to obtain a micro insurance licence and operate in the market, not only existing insurance companies."[72]

FREEMIUM

It's here that we can address the 'freemium' model, which fits in very well with microinsurance. It's not just a financial issue that limits the world's poor to access the banking enablers of the modern world, but it's also the lack of a historical understanding (which we've discussed) and ultimately a lack of access. As I've said elsewhere, familiarity does not breed contempt with financial services, but rather comfort and confidence. The question is this: how do you introduce what is ultimately a complex product to an unsophisticated audience, who don't believe they need the product just because they've never used it before? As we've discussed, bundle it with a more advanced service they do use —but rather than ask them to pay for it, give it to them for free.

---

71 See KPMG, *Microinsurance supports improved financial inclusion in South Africa*, available at www.sablog.kpmg.co.za/2014/01/microinsurance-supports-improved-financial-inclusion-in-south-africa/). Also see the South African Treasury's summary at http://www.treasury.gov.za/public%20comments/DraftInsuranceBill2015/Annexure%20B.pdf

72 Risk Africa Magazine. See www.risksa.com/micro-insurance-products-profitable-study/

This is what freemium is about. It's when basic services for a product are free while more advanced services and features can be paid for. The idea has actually mostly come from the mobile phone game market where you get the game for free but need to pay for extra bonus items, lives, or levels. Yes, Candy Crush has come to insurance, and it's working in a very interesting way. In fact, any service that provides something for free and asks for payment for a more premium version, is essentially using the freemium concept. Gmail, Dropbox, Skype, are testimonies of how freemium can create success.

GHANA LEADS THE GAME

I first came across the freemium concept with Tigo Ghana in a report from GSMA[73] and I was totally enamoured by it. In a time when most mobile operators were looking to drive new products and services, Tigo Ghana came up with a very simple concept that not only improved customer loyalty but was actually a product the customer wanted. The concept now seems so logical, so obvious; but trust me, at the time it was ground-breaking. Ground-breaking enough for me to reach out to the then Head of Mobile Financial Service at Tigo Ghana (now Chief Operating Officer, COO at Digicel Group), Selorm Adadevoh to find out how he came about the concept. It was a group effort, but I believe he was the one with the guts to take a fresh new approach.

Tigo Family Care Insurance in Ghana is a free product on Tigo voice customers who use a certain amount of airtime in a month. But customers can effectively double their coverage for an additional fee of US$ 0.68 per month. The idea is simple: intro-

---

73   GSMA, *2014 State of the Industry: Mobile Financial Services for the Unbanked*. Available at www.gsma.com/mobilefordevelopment/wp-content/uploads/2015/03/SOTIR_2014.pdf

duce customers to the product at no cost to them, and when they see the benefits they will be more agreeable to paying for it.

Like with mobile video games, the free version is not profitable, but there are other ways in which revenue comes in, such as encouraging customers to use more airtime. In Tigo's case, the more airtime you purchase, the more your cover increases. The interesting result was that during high travel times, when call volumes are actually at their highest, the highest life cover is achieved by customers.

To get this to work across the board, all that's needed is an application programme interface (API) which connects the network operator's system to the insurance underwriter's system. MicroEnsure provided this to Tigo. Network operators already have all the details the insurance company needs —customer details, access to their finances, and so on. Customers just need to opt in to the product —for free —and all this information is given to the insurance company.

Opting in is easy. A simple "yes" or "no" pop-up screen occurs when a customer purchases and activates airtime. By simply replying or tapping "yes" the cover is automatically triggered.

In this simple way, customers become familiar with the product and what insurance is really all about: helping to lift poor people from the poverty cycle. Denis Garand, a renowned consultant in the microinsurance industry, has said in several places that when he explains what microinsurance is to people he knows in the traditional insurance industry, a light comes on. "This is what insurance is all about!" they say to him, suddenly remembering the whole point of the business.

For such an easy solution, both the mobile service provider and the insurance company get a massive return. And so Tigo's freemium model for its product in Ghana has seen a great response. "Of a total 489,000 insurance subscribers, more than 55 percent are now signed up on the paying plan and the share is increasing. That means Tigo in a single year has gone from zero to 270,000 paying customers in a segment where only 7% previously had insurance," reports Peter Zetterli at cgap.org.[74] This was in 2013! Tigo says that its freemium model has undoubtedly been the driver behind this. It created a market when there actually wasn't one before —by simply giving it to people in the first place. And digital payment services are about creating new markets. Freemium provides the incentive by piggybacking off what people are already doing and delivering additional benefits.

Vodacom (Vodafone)'s Faraja insurance product in Tanzania, using the M-Pesa service, is another example of how much piggybacking can take place —and the benefits. It provides a funeral benefit for one month to registered customers who make a minimum of ten M-Pesa cash transactions. Usually the Faraja insurance product is a premium product. Now, however, people who are already using the M-Pesa service —seven million in Tanzania in 2015 —are introduced to insurance products. M-Pesa also now functions in seven different African countries, with people able to transact via M-Pesa between these countries. What a market to introduce your product to!

Traditional insurance companies will take some time to get their heads around this, which is why the innovation is often coming from unexpected quarters, but I think there are very interesting opportunities here. The freemium model used by Tigo in Ghana also provides one way in which insurance companies can educate the market on complex products. Tigo is so confident in this that it has expanded to Senegal and Mauritius.

---

74   Freemium: *Spawning An Insurance Market in Ghana* (2013). Accessed at www.cgap.org/ blog/freemium-spawning-insurance-market-ghana

Of course, how will a freemium product perform in a developed market? It's very hard to say.

THE FUTURE

When freemium comes to financial inclusion, it becomes especially powerful. It solves one of the biggest problems of why so many digital payment products can have such amazing technology but yet fail —because no one wants to use it and there's no real incentive. The issue is, they just need to try it once and then realise the amazing benefits. Most people actually don't realise the benefit of Dropbox until they've actually used it. Then they can't live without it! How many times have you read a quote from naysayers of new technology asking, "Why would I need that?" only for those products to become part of our everyday lives within a decade. The iPad, the iPod, and even the mouse are examples of this.

Microinsurance has seen some great success, although there have been significant challenges. On the positive side the market has increased from 78-million in 2007 to 500 million in 2015.[75] "This growth has been largely driven by both the active involvement of governments to better help citizens protect themselves against risks and the availability of payment systems, which has made it easier to collect premiums from low-income households and enabled a host of new players to get involved in micro-insurance."[76]

But Africa lags behind significantly when looking at the international market. Only 25 million are covered on the continent, despite the vast potential for this service. South Africa, Ghana,

---

75   (Source: CGAP; usb-ed.com.)

76   See University of Stellenbosch Business School (USB), *Africa provides vast potential for micro-insurance.* Accessed at www.usb-ed.com/content/Pages/Africa-provides-vast-potential-for-micro-insurance.aspx

Zimbabwe and Kenya are the key players where lessons can be learned. "Lessons can be drawn from South Africa's experience as an early mover with 8,2 million lives covered in 2009, as well as several other countries in Africa that are picking up steam in micro-insurance. These include Ghana, Zimbabwe and Kenya," says the University of Stellenbosch Business School.[77]

Craig Churchill, ILO Microinsurance Innovation Facility Team Leader, says learning from the experiences of practitioners and regulators in these countries, as well as drawing on key lessons from countries outside of Africa, will be fundamental in reaching the vast untapped market of Africa. Anja Smith, director of Cenfri, concurs, saying the keys lie in distribution channels: "Distribution partners in micro-insurance should not only sell policies and collect clients' money, but also allow clients to make changes to their policies and become the point where claims are paid. If not, we risk losing client value where it ultimately matters." Alternative distribution channels are key, and hence mobile money is a great alternative channel.

Opportunity comes through innovation and forward-thinking, which Tigo and Ghana serve as good examples. This model can be replicated across the continent and financial services markets as it speaks directly into Africa's context. Microinsurance, with its focus on creating localised products, can really tap into the market as the development of products that are beneficial to communities is key. As Denis Garand says, "Most important is to find the correct distribution method, and a product based on the inputs of the target market."

---

77   See University of Stellenbosch Business School (USB), *Africa provides vast potential for micro-insurance*. Accessed at www.usb-ed.com/content/Pages/Africa-provides-vast-potential-for-micro-insurance.aspx

"We think the next 15 years will see major breakthroughs for most people in poor countries. They will be living longer and in better health. They will have unprecedented opportunities to get an education, eat nutritious food, and benefit from mobile banking. These breakthroughs will be driven by innovation in technology -—ranging from new vaccines and hardier crops to much cheaper smartphones and tablets -—and by innovations that help deliver those things to more people.

—**Bill and Melinda Gates**

CHAPTER NINE

×

TOMORROW'S BANKS

T he quote above from Bill and Melinda Gates from their 2015 annual letter includes a prediction that almost everyone will have a mobile money account by 2030. It's summarised by this quote: "Mobile banking will help the poor transform their lives".[78]

They were speaking into the context that 2.5 billion people are unbanked in developed countries, who rely on informal financial services and cash. Both of these come with huge risks. Traditional banks don't help these risks but can increase them, plus they are expensive and very inconvenient. Thus traditional banks struggle to reach this market, particularly in rural areas.

But GSMA's stats show that, of these 2.5 billion people, over one billion have access to a mobile phone. That's why more than 250 mobile money services are in 89 countries by 2014. (Keep your eye on gsmaintelligence.com as new stats constantly get released.) Just decades ago banks had these major challenges

---

78   See *2015 Annual Letter* from Bill and Melinda Gates. Accessed at www.gatesnotes.
com/2015-annual-letter?lang=en&page=3

stated above when it came to selling and getting its products to end-users and consumers in developed-world contexts. But this has now changed. Unfortunately, too many banks don't even realise the change! As Chris Skinner, one of the world's best experts in digital banking states, the danger for banks is not digital, but not thinking.[79]

Skinner asks an interesting question at his blog (thefinanser. co.uk). In many developed world contexts technology has changed just about everything. From being able to see the entire world in our palm (Google Maps and Google Earth) to even hitching up our caravans to our cars using only a remote control app on our phone. But ten years ago, in many first-world countries, if you received a cheque you had to go to the bank and wait days for it to be cleared. Fast forward to 2015 and if you get a cheque, you have to go to the bank and wait days for it to be cleared. Nothing has changed! Why is that?

The reality is that it's often not the banks themselves that are pushing forward new technologies and ways of doing things, but other industries that are forcing banks to change. The mobile phone itself is a great example, while the M-Pesa service is also a case in point, which is helping to pave the way for a new wave of banking that is forcing traditional banks to catch up to technology, or be left behind. Here is a clear example of how the developing world's challenges have actually led to innovation. It's also a great example of how unexpected technologies are catalysts. One would think the banks themselves, driven by competition, would have been on the forefront of the change, but historically speaking that hasn't happened at all. In the Western world, interestingly enough, it's technology companies like Apple and Google who are almost forcing the hand of banks to change

79   See Chris Skinner's blog, *The danger for banks is not digital, but not thinking.* Accessed at thefinanser.co.uk/fsclub/2015/07/the-danger-for-banks-is-not-digital-but-not-thinking.html

and re-strategise. PayPal wasn't a bank's idea. I find this all very unexpected and interesting — and exciting.

AFRICA IS DIFFERENT

Of course I'm generalising, because banks in Africa and South Africa are actually quite at the forefront. As Ken Griffiths of ChamaPesa, an app we shall look at in greater detail in this chapter, says, "The environment that allowed M-Pesa to succeed in Kenya was largely due to the 'wait and see' policy of Kenya's Central Bank. The regulator is proud of their success and relatively permissive toward similar innovations. This is an encouraging environment for startups. Highly regulated developed countries tend to raise the barrier to entry for internet payment companies so high as to prevent innovation from getting started. For example, California is now claiming that AirBNB.com is a 'money transmitter' and must meet the same kind of licensure, ['know-Your-Customer' (KYC)] and reporting requirements as companies like Western Union. This type of over-regulation is driving innovators to the 'edges' of the developed world — places like Kenya — where there is more freedom to pursue new ideas."

So my criticism is more levelled at developed contexts, and part of this book is to show how Africa is innovating beyond these developed contexts. Many banks in America, to be quite frank, are simply taking ages to catch up. As Jean-Stéphane Gourévitch (a renowned expert in mobile banking) said at the UK's Fintech Week in 2015:

"When you look around the world you see that countries that have decided to maintain a monopoly from banks or have bank-led models have seen a very poor growth of mobile money in their region. Countries that have pushed a mixed model or an open model where any provider including mobile operators is able to provide mobile money directly, provided they obtained the necessary regulatory registration or licence, the growth rate is extraordinary."[80]

In speaking of Africa, Gourévitch notes that digital payment services didn't pick up in Western Africa as it did in Eastern Africa because Eastern Africa had buy-in and alignment from Central Banks who were keen to innovate and trial new developments without imposing immediate heavy banking regulations. The Ivory Coast and Ghana have seen tremendous growth in this field due to the way regulation has been approached.

"Safaricom's M-Pesa developed with Commercial Bank Of Africa — something called M-Shwari —that is an extraordinary proposition, which actually would be very useful in our developed countries for people that are unbanked or experiencing major financial woes," noted Gourévitch. M-Shwari is a savings and lending mobile money service which has seen tremendous success. We will also look at in more detail later in this chapter.

But what's interesting here is it's becoming a trend that people trust mobile service providers more than banks! This boils down not only to the actual technology but the perception of these companies: mobile telecommunications is visibly investing in African countries and its people, creating innovations that work for them, while traditional banks can often have a shady image of being inflexible and expensive. My experience in Africa has always been that people are asking the lingering question: "are you here to stay?" Traditional banks are not always showing

---

80   See International Business Times, *Why some banks and governments still stifling the mobile money inclusion miracle.* Accessed at www.ibtimes.co.uk/some-banks-governments-still-stifling-mobile-money-inclusion-miracle-1519716

that they are. And what do banks really provide to an African urban or rural context? As Gourévitch says, creating products that take into account the local conditions is what is making mobile money a winner. Even the weather has to be taken into account! "Weather patterns can influence whether it's possible or easy to provide mobile money because you are using frequencies and when you have monsoon rains or certain type of weather patterns, it creates interference so it is difficult to have any form of communication."

USER-CENTRIC APPROACH

So traditional banks have to change, and fundamentally. Even when it comes to corporate banking, a user-centric approach is winning. Mobey Forum, a global industry association which consults to banks around digital payments services, looked at 79 banks in the world and came out with some key findings for the corporate space. "The world is changing rapidly and the pressure on corporate finance departments to keep pace with enterprise mobility is growing," says Petra Bunschoten, Chair of the Mobile Corporate Banking Workgroup at Mobey Forum and Principal Consultant at ING Netherlands. "This is a real opportunity for banks, as long as they can optimise their services for the range of different mobile environments in use today. The holy grail lies in their ability to provide a consistent and convenient corporate banking service experience across all devices, from anywhere and at any time."

The point here is to show that mobile money solutions will soon enter this fray as innovation goes on. At the moment mobile money is not really competition, but it could be in due time. Why do I say that?

WORLDREMIT

A curious example comes from WorldRemit, a London-based service that lets people send money overseas using mobile money, rather than the traditional —and expensive —agents. Money can be received as a bank deposit, a cash pick-up, mobile money or even an airtime top-up. It's available to senders over 50 countries currently and offers transfers to over 120 countries, including Europe, Asia, North America, Asia and, of course, Africa.

The company has managed to raise $147 million from only four investors. Its founder and current SEO is a Somali, Ismail Ahmed, who remembers the days when it would take three months for a payment to arrive in Africa. "International remittances to mobile money are growing exponentially, not only across sub-Saharan Africa but in Asian and Latin American markets too. We're working hard to connect with all mobile money services around the world and see mobile-to-mobile remittances as at the very core of our business," he says.

Moni technologies, a London-based organisation, is another example. "Mobile money services enable financial inclusion and allow the poor to transform their lives. This is especially true in the remittance industry, where mobile money reduces the cost of making these transfers considerably. These services are creating products for the under and unbanked, something that was unimaginable a few years ago," says Laurence Aderemi, CEO and Co-Founder, Moni Technologies.

Paypal is, of course, another example of this kind of disruption. It's only a matter of time before this becomes something other businesses want to tap into, and in a big way. It provides the kind of technology many businesses need.

MFS AFRICA

But the most fascinating international remittance provider for me so far has to be Mobile Financial Services (MFS) Africa — which has successfully connected the five major mobile operators on the continent (MTN, Vodafone, Airtel, Orange and Tigo) and other licensed financial institutions together. Essentially, digital payments services are now speaking with each other, allowing for you to transfer from one to the other or to or from a traditional financial institution — across borders. In my chapter on Tanzania, one of its key growth drivers has precisely been interoperability. MFS Africa takes it one step further, by providing a platform for this kind of interoperability on a much larger scale.

Speaking to the CEO, Dare Okoudjou on my innovation radio segment, one gets the sense that this is truly an African innovation created by an African, and has a long life span in Africa. This is because it addresses the growth of digital payments services in the continent and takes it that "one step" it has needed to go.

LISTEN TO OUR INNOVATION SLOT WITH MFS AFRICA

All customers have to do is access the service via a USSD menu (so it works on very basic phones) and enter the beneficiary phone number, the transfer amount in their local currency, and then confirm the transaction (it will show them the amount in the currency of the beneficiary). Instantly the mobile money is transferred, while MFS Africa handles fees between the digital payment services.

A 30-person startup in Johannesburg is connecting 55 million people in 17 African countries. MFS Africa is doing more than just connecting these accounts, however, but is now selling health and life insurance through it. It's a clear example, to me, of the ecosystem I've been talking about —of how digital payment services bring it all together — the water in our coffee; the water in our innovation space.

It's also an example of how digital payment services are reaching into traditional banking markets. Traditional banks who see the opportunity here are partnering with digital payment services to do this.

AIRTIME REMITTANCE GIFTS

TransferTo is another company that amazes me with its out-of-the-box thinking. CEO, Eric Barbier saw an opportunity with international migrant workers who had to send money back home. The problem is that the cost of sending small amounts of money makes it counter-productive. Try sending the equivalent of $5 via a traditional money transfer operator. You'll quickly find out that it's a very expensive exercise, and the fees are much more than just the $5 amount you're trying to send! So what happens is most migrant workers have to save for weeks or months to make the cost of sending practical and affordable.

However, most of the family members actually need the $5 now, not in weeks or months. TransferTo saw this, thought outside the box, and said: "Instead of sending money back home, why not allow consumers to top up a phone with airtime, goods or services, or mobile money?"

From your phone you can top up your family's phone with any one of these, to the value of the money you are sending. "Goods and services" includes paying for groceries, a utility bill, education, public transport, healthcare, or even entertainment. For example, you buy a Pick 'n Pay grocery store voucher worth $2.50 and then select the number you want to send this voucher to. They receive the voucher which gives them a code they can use at a cashier. It happens over SMS, USSD, or even on the web.

Payment can happen from another digital payment service or from a traditional financial institution. NGOs can use the service too. TransferTo boasts of over 400 mobile operators working with it, and over a thousand building payment solutions with TransferTo — from online services such as Paypal and Xoom to more traditional services like Western Union, to grocery stores and banks, across the U.S., Africa, Latin America and the Caribbean, Asia Pacific, Europe, and the Middle East.[81]

Think of being able to buy a grocery voucher for practically anyone in the world, from your mobile phone, with no registration required. We're living in a new world, folks.

Here's one thing about TransferTo that I think companies should take note of, especially if they want to help with financial inclusion and provide additional value to your employees. Why not offer your employees the ability to send a fixed or flexible amount of their salary straight to their family every month, in the form of mobile money or any one of these services? The technology is there, and it will certainly increase the happiness of your employees. Your company could play a big part in providing microinsurance to your employee's family's farm in Ghana, somewhere. It's a very interesting prospect and helps bring the financial inclusion dream to more of a reality.

---

81 See www.transfer-to.com/services

MOBILE SAVINGS

But there's more. Access to savings at traditional, formal financial institutions can be very limited for the world's low-income population, which means that there are usually alternative methods that come with tremendous risk. A study recently showed that 75 percent out of 1,232 Ugandans who saved by investing in commodities or animals or other goods lost some of their savings. Also, given that low-income households tend to stow cash under mattresses or somewhere in the house, this money is usually much more easily spent, not to mention easily stolen. It's interesting how having a bit of cash lying around makes us spend it, whereas having it stored somewhere else makes it less easy to spend. Plus carrying cash around makes one a target.

Digital payment services offer a way in which the money isn't 'there', even though it can be so easily accessed. That's why the unbanked find mobile savings attractive as it increases access and minimises risk. Of course, savings and security are two of the main reasons people bank at all. Digital payment services are increasingly showing benefits in both of these spheres.

According to the GSMA's State of the Industry 2014 —Mobile Financial Services for the Unbanked report,[82] financial services companies and mobile operators are increasingly making use of mobile money infrastructure to offer savings facilities. George Bedo, head of banking research at Ecobank, which has also rolled out a mobile-based savings and credit service, says there is huge potential in this sphere. "It is estimated that there is $1.2bn in cash stuffed under mattresses or in biscuit tins across Africa. If these funds could be leveraged through mobile banking, they could transform lending to local businesses, which currently pay

---

82   GSMA, *2014 State of the Industry: Mobile Financial Services for the Unbanked.* Available at www.gsma.com/mobilefordevelopment/wp-content/uploads/2015/03/SOTIR_2014.pdf

exorbitant interest rates," he says.[83]

There is opportunity here because there are not too many services like this… yet. But regulators need to be encouraged. The governor of the National Bank of Rwanda, Rwangombwa John, sees the potential:

> "The ultimate goal is to use these mobile financial services to start creating savings. This supports the ultimate aim of financial inclusion… but also poverty reduction," he says. "Going forward, we are going to have savings on the mobile services that are linked to micro-loans, so it is going to have an even bigger impact on the lives of the population," he says.

As technology becomes cheaper and more complex, it will be easier for money providers to create new services. Plus, the ability to analyse people's spending habits and credit-worthiness will become much more sophisticated and efficient. And so, what started as a peer-to-peer money transfer service is now developing into something much more complex. Anybody in banking should immediately see the opportunity here. Mobile money accounts are increasingly being used to store cash, with 54.5 percent of accounts enjoying a positive balance (as from June, 2014). It's not only savings but also credit that is starting to happen through digital payments services.

As an example, we've discussed Tigo Tanzania's very unexpected move in this space previously. To briefly recap, Tigo pays out interest to customers using its mobile money service. The result has been an 11 percent net increase in 'cash-ins' (September 2014 numbers show $8.7 million (USD) in interest was given to

83 See This is Africa, *Mobile money: The next generation.* Accessed at www.thisisafricaonline. com/News/Mobile-money-The-next-generation?ct=true

3.5 million users, and then a further $1.8 million in November.) For many, the pay-out is actually quite substantial when looking at their income.

Tigo partners with Tanzania's central bank, which brings investment and savings services to mobile money —with the huge potential of enhancing financial inclusion with the 'bottom of the pyramid'.

Airtel Uganda, which partners with the Grameen Foundation, serves as another example —and one which understands the local context. Here groups of people can store their group's cash as mobile money. Three members of the group must enter three different PINs to unlock the cash. When the cash is unlocked, all members in the group are sent an SMS. This offers a great deal of transparency and security, and Airtel's research shows that adopters are also now more inclined to use other services since trying this one out. Airtel is making great strides in the mobile money arena. All one has to do is look at Chidi Okpala's (Director and Africa Head, Airtel Mondy) Linkedin profile[84], to see almost weekly press releases on a new product or country where they've rolled out mobile money. Aggressive roll out is brilliant for the portion of the 2.5 billion unbanked in Africa.

WHATSAPP FOR MONEY

Informal social fundraising is quite popular with lower income families and individuals. This is often preferable because it's done by fundraising with extended family, friends, and neighbours. The funds usually don't need to be repaid. Often weddings and funerals are paid for in this way.

But as increasing urbanisation happens, and people are further away from each other, this kind of fundraising has become more

---

84   www.linkedin.com/in/chidi-okpala-8395156

difficult. Fortunately, technology is able to connect us in new ways, and here we've seen something new emerge.

M-CHANGA AND CHAMAPESA

M-Changa in Kenya digitises the social fundraising idea, using the local context and mobile money services. It's an app which allows you to manage a fundraiser through it. "M-Changa's 10,000 customers have raised $180,000 through 65,000 customer interactions via Safaricom's M-Pesa, Airtel Money, and PayPal," says the GSMA.[85] The data it generates also helps to analyse what motivates people to give, and how they like to give.

The ChamaPesa app, available in Kenya, is another route to providing mobile savings by assisting an existing local cultural system. In Kenya there are over 300,000 social savings groups (co-operative societies) called Chamas. It's like a micro-saving group which emerged in the late 1980's and 1990's, originally by women's groups. Chamas, although informal, are quite secure —in order to join, members must undergo an interview and have assurances from an existing member. Kenya's Chamas are recorded as saving about 300 billion shillings (that's US$ 3.4 billion) a year. The cash is stuffed in lock boxes and kept out of the formal system.

It is, of course, often mismanaged. ChamaPesa therefore provides Chamas with tools for better management, transparency and governance. It also allows for the formal sector to begin to tap into the Chamas, as through the app financial institutions can offer their financial services —currency accounts, insurance, securities, and so on. Plus it enables users to save into a Chama account using M-Pesa. Hence the name.

---

85   GSMA, *2014 State of the Industry: Mobile Financial Services for the Unbanked.*

ChamaPesa's Ken Griffith has been involved in the digital payments space since 1997. After reading The Sovereign Individual by James Davidson and Lord Rees-Mogg, which he says accurately predicted "the miracle of M-Pesa", he had the revelation that Internet-based payment systems would be the way the world would go. While the ChamaPesa Android app is focused on savings, Griffith says it is fundamentally a payment system that is network independent —and therein lies the key to its future success, and a future opportunity for entrepreneurs. "Samsung and Intel are saying that in five years the majority of Africans will have Android phones. This will open the door for payments apps like ChamaPesa that work for people using different telephone companies, and could allow the Kenyan diaspora to use the same payment application as their family in Kenya. Imagine "WhatsApp" for money."[86]

In other words, an app like ChamaPesa is able to work around several issues with regards to legislation and interoperability. Griffith says his hope is that the long-term impact of this work will be able to raise the savings rate in Africa. "We believe the reason for relatively low savings rates in Africa is partly because the poor do not have a way to save that gives them real returns after inflation. By giving the poor better quality savings options, we think we can increase the incentive for people to save."

IT'S NOT COMPETITION

As Jean-Stéphane Gourévitch said at the UK's Fintech Week in 2015, this all shows how digital payment services are growing. "In

---

86   See Venture Capital for Africa (VC4A), FUNDRAISING: CHAMAPESA, KENYA'S NEW MOBILE SAVINGS SYSTEM. Accessed at vc4africa.biz/blog/2013/08/26/fundraising-chamapesa-kenyas-new-mobile-payment-system-providing-multiple-financial-instruments/

a number of countries in Africa and Asia you can also pay directly your rent to your landlord, you can pay utilities, proceed to a number of banking operations, saving, even insurance through your mobile — it's not just transfer or remittance anymore but a more sophisticated financial services ecosystem and in some respect more advanced than in developed countries."

Mobile operators are in the fortunate position of being able to process large amounts of small transactions, which traditional banks find costly. This is why mobile savings is not seen to compete with but rather enhance traditional banking, creating new banking opportunities.[87]

Credit and savings can effectively work together in digital payment services, aiming these two services at the same customers, and using the same pool of money. Savings enables credit. It helps people to demonstrate their credit-worthiness. There has been a marked increase in mobile credit services —as much as 50 percent in 2014 (as per the GSMA). This has occurred due to new partnerships with mobile operators and banks to bring mass-market short-term loans, as well as microfinance institutions and startups looking to target specific groups.

INVENTURE AND M-SHWARI

Now comes the fun part. In order to provide credit to a customer, not only do you have to have some form of credit history, but you also have to show proof of income, proof of residence and valid identification. For most of the unbanked population in Africa, getting two out of the three is almost near impossible, which means they are disqualified before they even begin.

InVenture and M-Shwari are two innovative platforms that seek to solve this problem. How? Through the purchase of

---

87   GSMA, *2014 State of the Industry: Mobile Financial Services for the Unbanked.*

airtime — something Africans have become accustomed to and generally have a monthly spend towards.

This is where InVenture and M-Shwari saw an innovative way to credit score individuals that couldn't qualify for traditional credit. By looking at the data already being collected on monthly airtime purchases of a customer, and looking at the data already being collected by mobile money accounts like M-Pesa, new credit scoring models and ways of measuring data are emerging. Using this data, InVenture and M-Shwari offer customers credit and investment schemes. The result? Lower numbers of non-performing loans compared to traditional loans. There are reasons for this, as we shall see. But what it means is that access to credit is opening up for many that would be first time formal borrowers and would previously have no access to such schemes.

Here once again, formal and traditional credit services, even those provided by microfinance institutions (MFI's) such as Amhara Credit and Savings Institution in Ethiopia, come to a limit in reach into low-income families and individuals due to products, a lack of flexibility, context etc. The informal sector, however, manages to surpass these challenges —but it is often very expensive when it comes to interest. Excessively. That's why, if people can borrow using a mobile credit service, both of these challenges are addressed.

Many mobile money providers don't have the legal ability, the funds, or expertise to get into credit, and thus they look to partner financial services and banks. This is an emerging trend. Worldwide, 37 such services are now active, many which operate in several countries. M-Shwari partners with both the Commercial Bank of Africa and Safaricom (a telecommunications provider). M-Pesa customers who have a good track record and payments history are able to get access to credit through the service, usually cheap short-term loans with an interest rate of 6 —7 percent.

But the M-Shwari savings account also enables users to purchase a smartphone if they've deposited 30 percent of the price of the device into their account. They must repay the loan within six months. This is Safaricom's side of the business, who would want to increase the proliferation of smartphones in their market (the stats show that smartphones grew 50 percent in 2014 in Kenya). By being able to take back the phone if the customer defaults, Safaricom also creates leverage for itself, keeping default rates lower than what a straight-up loan would do. You are effectively rewarded for saving money. In 2015 there were over 10 million M-Shwari accounts and 50,000 loans dispersed every day. On its own, M-Shwari has grown the number of borrowers in Kenya by 800 percent.[88] This made it Central Bank of Africa's largest retail lender. M-Shwari has helped M-Pesa and Central Bank of Africa realise that more savings products are needed, and so a six month fixed deposit savings account has also launched, based on the feedback that customers want a "facility which would inherently instil in them the discipline to make medium term savings towards a specific goal." (Ipsos report.) According to an earlier survey by InterMedia, 14 percent of M-Shwari customers used the service so they could save money and build a record to make a future purchase or payment. In other words, people actually want services that don't just give them access to finance, but help to educate them and build positive habits.

---

88   Source: Ipsos. See www.ipsos.co.ke/NEWBASE_EXPORTS/Airtel/140611_Business%20Daily_8.._7720f.pdf

OTHER SERVICES IN THE SAME SPACE

M-Shwari and InVenture's success has spawned several other services in what has become successful digital payment services spaces. In Tanzania, M-Pawa is a savings programme launched by Vodacom, partnered with Commercial Bank of Africa again. According to reports, it saw 250,000 new registered customers in its first three weeks![89] By the end of 2014, it had one million new customers —accordingly, one in five of Tanzania's M-Pesa users signed up. Like M-Shwari, M-Pawa allows users to save as little as a shilling and then borrow as per their credit history. Depositing and withdrawing money is free, using M-Pesa.

MoDe, launched in 2010 in Kenya, effectively provides "emergency credit" —turning "SIM cards into credit cards". When airtime runs low, customers get access to cashless credit so they can keep talking.[90] In Ghana, MFS Africa has launched Mjara Loans on the MTN network, giving MTN Mobile Money customers the ability to submit loan applications through the system and receive an instant response.

But it's not just end users who are benefiting, but also SME's and micro-merchants, as credit becomes available to companies. Kiva Zip, which was launched in 2011, is a peer-to-peer lending programme where micro loans are given to entrepreneurs in Kenya with zero interest and no fees. It also works through M-Pesa and has, to date, given over 5,000 loans. (About 40,000 individuals globally contribute into the programme.) Kopo Kopo is another example, which provides a merchant cash advance service called GROW that also measures the credit history of a business. Kopo Kopo has, up until 2015, managed to facilitate just more than US$ 2 million in cash advances to about 600 merchants.

---

89   Source: Ipsos. See www.ipsos.co.ke/NEWBASE_EXPORTS/Airtel/140611_Business%20 Daily_8.._7720f.pdf

90   See mo-de.co/company/

NEW DATA TRACKING

Then it's also banks that are benefiting. Microfinance and traditional banks have always faced the challenge of knowing whether a customer will pay or default on a loan. This very often affects the affordability of loans —they need to cover their risks somehow. But with big data and mobile provider data, including mobile money data now emerging, new credit-scoring algorithms are providing new insight. As I touched on a little earlier, the use of mobile telecommunications data for credit scoring has resulted in a lower number of non-performing loans (this means loans that have defaulted or are about to do so). Only 2.2 percent of M-Shwari loans are non-performing in 2014. This is partly driven by the fact that this is the first time many of these people have access to credit, and they want to pay it back so they don't lose this access. Also, good payment behaviour is rewarded —by reducing the interest rate, offering more data or airtime, or providing other products that we've discussed in this book. Offering airtime is often a great way of testing a customer's creditworthiness, before higher tier products are offered —for example, loaning a secured asset or unsecured cash via mobile money (which is high risk). By partnering with credit-scoring companies, telecommunications providers can provide great insights which can be gleaned from airtime top-up records, when people call or send SMS, payment histories, which phones are popular, social network usage, and so on.

THE BENEFITS ARE CLEAR

It's easy to see the trajectory here. What excites me is these innovations are coming from Africa. This is a continent leading the way in financial inclusion and the way banking might look in the future. If you didn't have a mobile money account before, now is the time to get on board!

"You can't create and capture the value for Africa. Only those who are really here for the long term can see beyond today's narrative and into the future where one billion people become connected, communicate and entertained in new exciting ways."
—**Jason Njoku, Founder of Irokotv**[91]

×

CHAPTER TEN

INNOVATION COMES TO ARTS AND ENTERTAINMENT

I t's easy to see how innovation in Africa, and how digital payment services, are working in the realms of business and practical, day-to-day needs. But what about arts and entertainment? After all, the continent is a huge basket of eclectic creativity, with enormous talent and amazing potential. Yet it seems it just can't tap into it effectively.

The arts and entertainment space in Africa gets a lot of support from governments and even corporations, but it is often, admittedly, less than other industries. Yet despite this support, arts and entertainment always seems to lack the grass-roots support that it actually needs to become a thriving sector.

The reasons for this are multifaceted and fairly obvious. According to Nicole Klassen, Head of Content at of Bozza.mobi, the challenges include geographical boundaries, limited access to resources and networks, and a lack of access to real revenue opportunities.[92] For me it ultimately comes down to three things:

---

a lack of expendable income, distribution challenges, and general public perception. On the industry's side, a lack of financial support can hinder the distribution and marketing required to compete against Western movies, musicians and performers, writers, poets, and even video games, and so on.

But things are changing, and in innovative ways. Perhaps the most dramatic change has been the rise and rise of the Nigerian film industry, affectionately called "Nollywood."

IROKOTV

We touched on Nigeria-based IrokoTV in a previous chapter. Since 1960, the Nigerian film industry has steadily increased, with a boom in the 90's that helped propel it to the second largest film industry in the world today — over 2000 titles made a year in 2013 — and the third most valuable.[93] Nollywood is about African stories told by African people in African ways for Africans, and it has expanded way beyond its borders, not only throughout Africa but also the Carribeans and African Diaspora. In fact, most of IrokoTV's audience is from the Diaspora.

In December 2010, Manchester University graduate Jason Njoku was asked by his mom to get him some Nollywood DVDs. Naturally, he googled where he could find them, thinking he would obviously find them online. But no luck. He knew how popular Nollywood is amongst African diasporans and that it was the world's second largest film industry, so he wondered why no one had thought of the obvious: to make it available online.

At the same time he had the eyes to see another trend — the exponential growth of Internet connectivity in Africa. This gave him an idea, so he got himself to Lagos and realised the oppor-

93   See Business Day, *Nollywood improves quality, leaps to N1.72trn revenue in 2013.* Accessed at businessdayonline.com/2013/12/nollywood-improves-quality-leaps-to-n1-72trn-revenue-in-2013/#.VFQINRYjQSY

tunity at his fingertips. From his two-bedroom apartment, he and a small team began to buy online licenses for Nollywood films and stream them on a dedicated YouTube channel called NollywoodLove. It soon had 1,100,000 viewers a month.

At this time Njoku was nearly broke. To fund the project, he used advertising, and advertised other Nollywood films, generating more interest. At the time, no one in the industry really considered the online avenue, relying on DVD's and suffering from a great deal of piracy, so to buy licensing was actually quite cheap (it's a whole different story today, thanks to Njoku's IrokoTV). The project attracted investment from a New York-based private equity firm (Tiger Global Management) to the total of $10 million. It soon became obvious that a more dedicated solution was needed, and there was money to build it, so IrokoTV was born. In 2012 another investment of $2 million came in.

Since then, the company has launched an app and partnered with global firms and broadcasters — supplying airlines with Nollywood content, signing distribution deals, and even expanding into traditional satellite broadcasting with two dedicated channels through a deal with Arica's Star Times. It also continues to make money through strategic advertising on the platform. Many of the movies are actually free, but subscribers to the IrokoTV Plus platform get to watch the latest releases or most popular movies. According to smallstarter.com[94], it's likely that the outfit could be making over $2 million a month on subscriptions alone, if those subscriptions are renewed (they may not be). If subscriptions are not renewed, it estimates about $200,000 a month. The answer is probably somewhere in-between.

In 2016, IrokoTV entered into a partnership with Netflix to distribute select Nollywood content to the American-based

---

94   See Smallstarter.com, www.smallstarter.com/get-inspired/iroko-tv/

platform. Obviously, Netflix understands there is a demand. (For the record, IrokoTV actually has more content movie-for-movie than Netflix's global catalogue). The point is this: an industry that traditionally was difficult to access for Africans in the Diaspora has been blown open by IrokoTV, where 55 percent of its audience comprises of subscribers from the US and UK. Njoku likes to talk about "setting Nollywood free". It's done that, and not only through its new distribution channel and reaching previously unreached audiences, but in other ways as well, which are important when we speaking of support for local arts and culture. As Njoku explains:

> "We've not only brought Nollywood to a much larger, global audience, but through our considerable investment, we've also helped to elevate the quality of what's now being released. Producers are now able to better monetise their content and can reinvest their higher profit margins into better facilities, equipment and so on.[95]"

IrokoTV's plan for 2016 has been to produce 300 movies, thanks to a 19 million dollar investment from the French media giant CANAL+ and existing investor Kinnevik AB. "We've also helped to elevate the quality of what's now being released," continues Njoku. "Producers are now able to better monetise their content and can reinvest their higher profit margins into better facilities, equipment and so on. I hope that we have had a positive effect on Nollywood, improving the industry for both producers / directors, as well as fans."

Nollywood is said to contribute to 1.4 percent of Nigeria's

---

95   See filmcontact.com, *Has Nollywood Streaming lost its appeal?* Accessed at www. filmcontact.com/news/nigeria/distribution/has-nollywood-streaming-lost-its-appeal%3F

GDP, a major employer in the country.[96] So support is there, it's growing, and the quality of the movies is increasing. All thanks to innovation. The innovation is not only the model, but also the technology. Because of traditional infrastructure challenges, iRokoTV has had to find ways to work in a bandwidth-light environment, and has been forced to optimise where services like Hulu and Netflix haven't had to. This, no doubt, will set precedents for other services like it in the future.

And Njoku is not in the least worried about Netflix being in Africa. "What iROKO is, and has largely always been known for, is the home of Nollywood. Home and abroad. The strange thing about the mourners of iROKO is they always mention how most of our subscribers are in the West. Yup US and UK represent ~55% of our subscription base. And it's grown (not break-neck) but steadily over the last few years, in Netflix's back yard. Folk in the US and UK (the top two Netflix markets) have been happy to pay YoY for the little service we provide. Building subscription businesses are hard. Heck we are only four years old," he said in an interview.[97] "If it's Nollywood fanatics, you know those guys can watch 3-5 hours per day, so Irokotv is still the only place they can find most of what they are looking for. Considering we are one of the biggest actual producers of Nollywood, I don't see that changing anytime soon. In time, we will be able to produce 200 movies a year ourselves, no shaking. And with the evident collapse of the DVD market, this only makes us stronger."

With the launch of an app, I can foresee, if any of the digital payment services are clever, subscriptions to IrokoTV-like

---

96   See the BBC, *'Nigeria's Netflix' takes Nollywood to a global audience.* Accessed at www. bbc.com/news/business-28528396

97   See TechZim, *CEO of iROKOtv "Africa's Netflix" shares thoughts on Netflix entering the continent.* Accessed at www.techzim.co.zw/2016/01/ceo-of-irokotv-africas-netflix-shares-thoughts-on-netflix-entering-the-continent/

services can be built in to the service. Often, in the States, if you sign on with a particular mobile operator, you receive access to streaming sports TV and other goodies. Why not do the same with IrokoTV? I realise it's difficult given the limitations in data costs, but it certainly would be a fantastic value-add service.

But it's not just the film industry that Njoku has been looking at. In 2013, Njoku and his co-founder of IrokoTV, Sabastian Gotter, founded an angel investment outfit in Nigeria called SPARK, which helps to fund young tech and Internet startups. It's provided funds to fifteen startup companies, of about $30 —$75k in total. And the year before that, Njoku launched Iroking.com, an online music streaming service that focuses on African artists and musicians. We'll look at music streaming in a moment, but for now I want to look at another TV innovation — Tuluntulu.

TULUNTULU.COM

Tuluntulu (meaning "stream" in Zulu), labelled one of the top 50 startups in the world by Unilever Foundry 50, and headed up by Pierre van der Hoven, brings traditional TV and radio to the mobile, allowing users in Africa to simply download the app and watch (or listen to) African-focused content anywhere. Two of its biggest drawing cards is that it's free and, secondly, it's designed to work on low bandwidth connections, with users given the option of setting up the quality of the video or radio stream. It can work seamlessly even on an EDGE connection! As Pierre discussed on my radio segment, EDGE uses less data, which makes Tuluntulu the cheapest way to watch TV.

> "We are the free-to-air for mobile in Africa," he says. "Our major markets are SA, including Nigeria, Ghana, Tanzania and Uganda. We have others in 154 countries who have

downloaded the app. We're probably the biggest app in Africa you haven't heard of."

LISTEN TO PIERRE VAN DER HOVEN DISCUSS TULUNTULU ON OUR INNOVATION RADIO SEGMENT.

Pierre comes from the TV industry and truly believes the future is digital. To reach an African market, the audience should not be excluded if they don't have a credit card or are not part of mobile money. This is why users can download the app from the iTunes or Google Play stores for free, and register for free for the service directly through Facebook. Tuluntulu's business model is based on advertising —advertisers are able to reach audiences through the app with many different forms of advertising, including the ability to survey users. Channels broadcast 24/7, and at the time of writing 20 video channels and 10 radio stations are on board — from sport to news (including Al Jazeera) to documentary channels, and Nolly4U, a Nigerian movie channel.

Charles Igwe, CEO of Nollywood Global and respected in the African entertainment space, has challenged the entertainment space in Africa to not only evolve, but to get content to audiences before outside producers do. "All content is going digital, there is therefore an explosion of film content, in all forms. Big telecoms companies will have to improve delivery and they will become broadcasters. Smartphones will get smarter, and fibre optic penetration will lead to higher bandwidth. Whose content will be inside those pipes? Creating the capacity to make content is imperative if we are going to exist in this space," he said at AfricaCom 2014.[98] The same has to happen, therefore, with the music industry. So let's look at that next.

MUSIC STREAMING IN AFRICA

I roking.com, which I mentioned earlier, is obviously not the only music streaming service in Africa, and there is a lot of competition in this area —especially as overseas outfits like Deezer and Simfy Africa have moved in. Nevertheless, the services cropping up from Africa themselves offer interesting alternatives, especially in the fact that they are often free and often focus on local artists over trying to compete with the massive catalogues of the overseas services.

Mkito.com is another such service, a Tanzania-based company which began its foray into the scene in 2014. About 90 percent of the music can be downloaded (you do have a monthly limit on downloads) —not streamed — while the other 10 percent must be paid for. The service supports itself and the artists through advertising and short messages before a track plays. What's also unique about the service is the free downloaded tracks usually include the advertising, but you can pay for the track without the advertising. It has had a lot of support from artists who are able to directly upload their tracks and sell them through the platform, or share in the advertising. Like most of these kinds of services, it also has a social network element where you can share your favourite tracks with friends.

Mdundo in Kenya works on a similar principle, except that

---

98   See Screen Africa, Content for Africa: a multi-billion dollar market. Accessed at www. screenafrica.com/page/news/mobile-tv/1649456-Content-for-Africa-a-multi-billion-dollar-market#.VtaY1EIaa01

users can upload music. Many of these users are artists themselves, uploading their tracks to the service. Downloads are free with no limits, but there is advertising, and around $3 a month gets you unlimited access with no advertising. About 70 percent of the company's revenue goes straight to the artist, and the pay-out to artist per stream is higher than Deezer's in 2015 (US$0.038 as opposed to US$0,0168).

Orin, launched in 2015 by Nigerian Entertainment Today (NET) magazine, looks to offer exclusive Nigerian and African music streaming content to its subscribers. It's not just music, but video as well that it's offering —including tracks that have never before been digitised. There are features to make it function like an online radio, and inbuilt social media functions where users can connect with friends and even artists. The app is available on just about every mobile platform.

Tigo, for its part, decided to partner with Deezer to provide Ghana and Tanzania with a catalogue of 36 million songs, while focusing on adding locally-produced content.

The point of these short examples is to show that Africans are looking for ways to compete against their overseas competition by providing more targeted, local content, in local ways —for example, downloading costs less data in the long run than streaming songs. Offering free songs with advertising helps to provide support to artists who might otherwise receive very little support at all, due to the expendable income people have.

Music streaming is in its early days, and it's questionable how sustainable these services will be given the high costs and the comparatively little money actually going to artists. By offering more to artists, however, these services get better support from the artists themselves (who will advertise them) and they get better access to artist's catalogues. I find these projects interesting given how they are not trying to copy what we see overseas. But more innovation is required. That's why I think, from an artist and support for the artist's perspective, where things really get interesting is in a service such as Bozza, which we will look at next.

BOZZA.MOBI

"Art plays the most fundamental role in culture — in our art we can really begin to remember who we are," says Emma Kaye, founder and CEO of Bozza.mobi, a mobile-first digital marketplace for the pan-African entertainment and media industry. Bozza basically allows for artists to directly connect with fans — but more than MySpace has ever really provided in the past, and uniquely African.

With the rise of the African middle class, the media and entertainment industry is enjoying much more support on the continent. Despite that the continent is only providing one percent to the global creative economy, according to UNESCO, South Africa's media and entertainment industry is estimated to be worth 17.4 billion by 2017. That's only South Africa, so what about the rest of the continent?

Africa is in the unique place to once again leapfrog traditional modes of doing things in the arts and entertainment space, and doesn't need to go through the rigmarole of an entire industry's business being uprooted for the new.

Artists upload their work to the Bozza platform —be it music, videos, poetry, or photos, and revenue is created both on and off the platform. On the platform, users access a digital store where they can communicate directly with the artist, and artists receive revenue from advertising. Off the platform there are opportunities with publishing deals (Bozza has a royalty publishing deal with music artists) and the ability to synchronise artists and channels together. There is also the ability to advertise events and engage in opportunities that come your way as you reach a certain level on the site.

"On Bozza every view and share counts towards real services that you can use to further advance your career. Opportunities, services and financial opportunities are featured on the site. This initial offer includes services like mixing & mastering, digital campaigns, and video production for creatives who achieve a target number of views & shares," says the company.

But what has also really impressed me is the innovation of creating an SMS sales code platform in South Africa for musicians and filmographers. All these artists have to do is request Bozza to set it up at no charge. An SMS code is a short keyword that customers send to a particular number which then purchases the item for them. For example, the artist Rheebongs can tell his fans to SMS the word Vuka to 37616 to buy his song titled Vuka. An amount of R7.50 will be deducted directly from his customers' airtime. Artists get 70 percent revenue from that after the operator and intermediary costs are deducted. On average, an artist therefore receives R2.14 for every R7.50 sold. Earnings are paid directly into the artist's bank account.

I was really impressed with this as it provides an easily accessible, and rather African solution, to creating a revenue stream, given how prolific SMS is across the continent. It's an example of digital payment services, of course. And it can be set up at the click of a few buttons! Given that Bozza accepts all genres in all African languages, it's a platform that begins to show just how far we've come in realising that our artists are actually brilliant, and it helps for us to see that in an accessible, tangible way. Mobile is also considered to be the first port of call for media and entertainment across the world, and here is a platform doing things differently.

BUNI MEDIA

Maria Lora-Mungai, often called a 'serial media entrepreneur', fits into a similar space as IrokoTV, except directly into the creative sector. She is considered a pioneer by many, founding Buni Media in Kenya.

She actually began her career as a journalist for CNN, BBC and Reuters. She moved to Kenya in 2006 on the gig of being a foreign correspondent in journalism, travelling to about 15 countries on the continent.

> "[I covered] the usual conflicts, elections and disasters. But what I was most interested in was the economic boom that I could see coming at the horizon, way before any talk of 'Africa Rising'," she says at Africandigitalart.com.[99]

Much like myself, she started hearing about African entrepreneurs, pioneers, and creatives who were innovating in new and interesting spaces. She began to focus on these stories of innovation. After meeting Gado, a well-known editorial cartoonist in Kenya, together they launched a political satire show called the XYZ Show (which currently has an audience of 10 million through online, TV and radio channels), which makes use of caricatured puppets.

The show was so successful that they started producing other

---

99   See African Digital Art, INTERVIEW WITH MARIE LORA-MUNGAI FOUNDER OF BUNI MEDIA. Accessed at africandigitalart.com/2014/01/interview-with-marie-lora-mungai-founder-of-buni-media/

kinds of media content, including animation, fiction films, children's shows, and so on.

But how did they raise the money? By her own admission, this is difficult in Africa, especially in her field. By looking at grants from foundations, they began to fund the company. Then, finding the right people was guided by an intern programme. Every year they take in 15 to 25 young interns, train them, and hire the best of them. Many of these young interns have been promoted quite extensively within two years.

Buni Media has brought an interesting development in distributing creative content throughout Africa. It's here where mobile came in, as this is where she saw a new, exciting, and accessible distribution platform. Buni Media was then conceptualised as a web and mobile video-on-demand (VOD) platform for high quality African content.

"Africa is a place where everybody thinks out of the box," she says. "People have to because very often the support infrastructure is not there, so you have to make your own way. That's one of the reasons I believe Africans are hyper-creative, and this has the potential to give Africa an edge in the global economy."

The creative space isn't easy in cultures that would rather spend money on tangible things they can use. But Lora-Mungai has noticed a certain trend developing. Most Africans, she says, used to spend their extra money on Western products, believing they were always better. That happens a lot less now. "'Made in Africa' is going to become people's first choice," she says. I think she's right —Nollywood and platforms like Bozza are showing this to be the case.

VIDEO GAMES

I'm now going to devote a short space to talk about an industry most people don't consider when speaking about Africa: video games.

It might surprise you to learn that the world wide video game industry is actually estimated to be worth more than the movie (box-office ticket sales) and music industry combined. Bear in mind, it's quite a young industry compared to these two stalwarts. It's safe to say it has an amazing future ahead of it.

But have you ever wondered what it would be like to be the first of a particular industry in a country? Eyram Tawia and Wesley Kirinya have an idea on that — the founders of the first successful game development studio in Ghana, Leti Games. According to them, African game development is certainly emerging. Overall, Leti is only the second full-time game development studio in all of Sub-Saharan Africa, if you exclude South Africa.

Their first released game, iWarrior, was on the iPhone, where players protect a village from wild animals (in a Space Invaders style). To help build it, they came up with two ideas. One, an internship program with high-schoolers and students, where they teach the basics in making games (modelling, story writing, animation, programming, and games engines). But the other challenge they found was how to get people to buy it, because a simple credit card debit poses a problem for Africans who are not buying into the traditional banking system.

So what did they do? Well, they turned to digital payment services, of course. Some studios and distributors have tried to make use of digital payment services in the past, but the cultural differences are often a clear problem. For example, Resident Evil 5 —developed by a Japanese studio —didn't fly very well when part of the game involved slaughtering spear-wielding warriors in villages.

For their part, Leti believes that African games made by Africans in African settings will be far more successful in Africa. But they're not setting their sights only on Africa. "Our focus is to make games from Africa for the world," says Tawia. Its other game, Ananse: The Origin features an African trickster god in a comic story. That kind of story also garners international interest because the medium and the story itself is something Westerners would typically be interested in as well.

Gamsole, from Nigeria, is another success story in-the-making. From 2012 to 2015, it has created over 35 titles, and (at the time of writing) has enjoyed over 15 million downloads of its games. The studio also hires itself out for animation projects. Through advertising and selling the games, it has managed to fund itself and do very well. Abiola Olaniran, founder of the company (who is on Forbes' "30 Most Promising Young Entrepreneurs In Africa 2015" list)[100] says, "Our goal is to make games that are fun to play; plain and simple. Each game offers a widely imaginative and irresistibly fun game-play experience that appeals to gamers of all age groups." Part of the company's strategy has been to focus on the Windows Phone store, where competition is significantly less.

CHALLENGES

The challenges for arts and entertainment in Africa remains a tough nut to crack. I can see how the advent of mobile technology and digital payment services can help in a big way. Some of the dots still need to be put together, especially from an industry perspective, and from creative entrepreneurs. But perhaps the biggest challenge has always been perception —that so many Africans feel that Western entertainment is better than African

---

100 See Forbes, *30 Most Promising Young Entrepreneurs In Africa 2015*. Accessed at www. forbes.com/sites/mfonobongnsehe/2015/02/05/30-most-promising-young-entrepreneurs-in-africa-2015/3/#150c71ce1bef

entertainment. This perception has a lot to do with budget, to be quite frank, and as technology makes it easier for content to get to an audience, the perception will change over time —I'm sure of it. But the perception starts with you. When you find out just how much Africa is producing, and just how good it really is, trust me, you will find yourself unwrapping a whole new world.

"When I was travelling through Africa last year what I heard was the desire of Africans not just for aid, but for trade and development that actually helps nations grow and empowers Africans for the long term… We recognise Africa for its greatest resource, which is its people and its talents and their potential."

- Barack Obama, President of The United States.

CHAPTER ELEVEN

AFRICAN ENERGY INNOVATION

A n efficient, reasonably-priced energy system greatly contributes to a better quality of life. It helps to unlock and improve healthcare, education, business, and even entertainment. It's a core component of any kind of developmental growth in a nation.

In 2014, the International Energy Agency noted that sub-Saharan Africa is especially facing challenges in this arena. More than 620 million people live without access to electricity, while 730 million use hazardous and inefficient solutions for things such as cooking and lighting, and so on. Those that do have access face increasingly rising prices, and the supply is often unreliable or inefficient. The International Energy Agency believes that Sub-Saharan Africa's existing energy resources are actually sufficient to meet its needs, but the problem lies in uneven distribution. "Sub-Saharan Africa is already home to several major energy producers, including Nigeria, South Africa and Angola, and these are being joined by emerging producers, including Mozambique and Tanzania," says its Africa Energy Outlook report.[101] "African countries more generally are endowed with abundant renewable energy potential, which they can harness so that, by 2040, renewables provide more than 40% of all power generation capacity in the region, varying in scale from large hydropower dams to mini- and off-grid solutions in more remote areas."

In 2011, the World Bank declared 32 of Africa's 48 nations to be in an energy crisis. Energy development has simply not coincided with the rapid development of the continent in other spheres. The high cost of what I could call traditional energy sources makes for a big challenge. It all requires significant investment.

But a question frequently arises, and continues to arise, and that is: should there be investment in traditional energy resources? Or should we be looking elsewhere? There are reasons for this question, of course: environmental concerns and cost being the big two.

I'm optimistic. The reason why is because I've seen so much innovation from Africa, that I'm quite convinced an interesting solution will be found. Interesting solutions are already being found, actually, sending us on an innovative trajectory. Again, we're sitting in a place where we can bypass the traditional approaches for the new. And why not? I'm not advocating we shouldn't pursue any kind of traditional infrastructure, but rather I'm saying there's no reason to put all of our eggs in one basket. Africa might just actually represent what the future needs to look like in terms of energy: clean, efficient, cheap, and accessible just about anywhere.

Let's look at several interesting startups that have been making waves in the Africa energy scene.

---

101   See International Energy Agency (IEA), *Africa Energy Outlook*, available at www.iea.org/publications/freepublications/publication/WEO2014_AfricaEnergyOutlook.pdf

M-KOPA SOLAR

M-Kopa Solar is my favourite African innovation of 2015. In chapter 3 I briefly mentioned M-Kopa solar, a pay-as-you-go off-the-grid solar option from Kenya, when I was speaking about how Africans are finding ways to bypass traditional infrastructure and how digital payment services are helping for that to happen. It would be appropriate, therefore, to look at M-Kopa in more detail here.

Without repeating myself here, the system essentially uses M-Pesa to help people pay just a little bit of money every day to rent a solar panel until they have paid it off. Essentially users start with a deposit of $30, and the payments are $0.50 a day. After paying it off, which usually takes a year, they own the solar panel and therefore actually enjoy free electricity. They also have the option of upgrading their power. If they don't pay, however, the device can be deactivated using GSM.

While the solar panels don't produce enough energy to supply a typical European or American household, they are enough to create a significant change in the lives of people who use them. Instead of resorting to kerosene or a wood fire for cooking and lighting, people can rather use clean electricity harnessed from the sun. Kerosene lamps are not only dangerous, but the fumes are actually hazardous to health. Even more, the daily payments of $0.50 a day is actually less than it would cost to keep the kerosene lamps burning!

Once users are finished paying off their first solar power device, they have access to several home-improvement and technology products, all using the mobile payments and GSM-enabled model. The products include lighting, energy-efficient cooking stoves, water tanks, and smart phones, plus more to come. "Delivering the promise of a better future for our customers is at the heart of what we do," says Moore. "It is great that customers with a responsible payment history can use their solar home systems to access practical products that help them get ahead.[102]"

The payments of the products are the same as the solar product ($0.50 a day), while there are different lengths of payment. This is all managed via the control panel on the original solar home systems.

The most popular of these products are the energy saving stoves, which are also locally manufactured. These use 50 percent less resources while being able to cook twice as fast. M-Kopa has even launched an off-the-grid digital TV set running entirely on solar! According to the Kenya Audience Research Foundation 2015 establishment data, TV only reaches 31 percent of the adult population on a daily basis. This leaves 69 percent of adults in the 'dark', who either lack access to power or simply cannot afford a TV set. M-Kopa's own customer research shows that over 80 percent of M-Kopa customers are very interested in acquiring solar TV, with the primary reason being so that their families can learn more about the world.[103] Jesse Moore, CEO at M-Kopa says owning a TV is life-changing for off-grid customers. "Many of them have traditionally had to pay to watch in a café or bar, or missed out on news and current events because they could not afford to be connected to information. We are now going beyond the grid to offer TV to homes all over Kenya. It's great for the family to be able to watch together in the comfort and safety of their home."

The upshot of using digital payment services and M-Kopa together is it obviously helps financial inclusion in other ways.

---

102   See CIO East Africa, *M-KOPA branches out with practical products.* Accessed at cio.co.ke/news/top-stories/m-kopa-branches-out-with-practical-products

103   See M-Kopa's press release at www.m-kopa.com/press-release/m-kopa-launches-solar-powered-tv/

Paying off a solar panel increases credit rating, instils a certain kind of discipline, exposes people to technology, and helps to change mindsets around credit, opening up easier discussion when it comes to less tangible products like insurance.

Smartphones are also one of M-Kopa's home improvement solutions that are quite popular, and what's interesting about that is it further brings digital payment services to the household, increasing financial inclusion and opportunity. One student, Felix Ogutu, got a smartphone through the M-Kopa programme and is now developing mobile phone applications![104]

M-Kopa's plans are to reach one million homes in East Africa with solar energy by the time 2017 ends. It is 280,000 in by 2015, covering Kenya, Tanzania and Uganda. All this in just three years. "We are just getting started," says Jesse Moore, chief executive officer (CEO) and co-founder of M-KOPA Solar.[105]

M-Kopa's funding comes from its sales but also regular funding rounds. In 2015 it managed to raise $19 million in its latest funding round. Before that, it's raised $12.45 million and $20 million. Al Gore has been part of the process, as well as Richard Branson and Jean and Steve Case (founders of AOL). It has also begun a training and development programme, funded by winning the Zayed Future Energy Prize ($1.5 million), called M-Kopa University.

---

104 See CIO East Africa, *M-KOPA branches out with practical products.* Accessed at cio.co.ke/news/top-stories/m-kopa-branches-out-with-practical-products

105 See Disrupt Africa, *M-KOPA Solar raises $19m.* Accessed at disrupt-africa.com/2015/12/m-kopa-solar-raises-19m/

M-KOPA RAISES $19M FOR AFRICA EXPANSION —
LISTEN TO THE NEWS REPORT.

OFF GRID ELECTRIC

Off Grid Electric uses a similar model to M-Kopa, with its latest funding seeing $45 million raised.[106] Altogether, it managed to raise $70 million in one year, with investment from Western Technology Investment, SolarCity, Omidyar Network, Serious Change LP, Vulcan Capital and the private investment firm of Microsoft co-founder Paul Allen.

According to Nancy Pfund, a managing partner of DBL Partners, a venture capital firm, this kind of funding helps to build the region's solar market in significant ways. "The fact that Off Grid Electric was able to put together a traditional, off-balance-sheet, non-recourse loan fund in a decidedly non-traditional market like Tanzania speaks volumes about what is going on in the region. As the installations funded by these pioneers come on-line and grow in numbers, the field will be de-risked, and we will see more traditional financial players enter as well." She sees this as not only about clean and affordable energy, but also job creation.

Off Grid Electric works closely with the Tanzanian govern-

---

106   See GTM, Off Grid Electric Raises $45M in Debt for African Micro-Solar Leasing Platform. Accessed at www.greentechmedia.com/articles/read/Off-Grid-Electric-Raises-45M-in-Debt-For-African-Micro-Solar-Leasing-Platf

ment to help reach the goal of powering up one million homes by 2017. It also has its sights set on Rwanda.

> "We have pioneered a business model that allows consumers with no formal credit to use their existing energy budget to finance solar. We simply redirect funds they were already paying for kerosene and batteries to a solar lease payment," says Xavier Helgesen, CEO and co-founder. He sees it as creating a new asset class of institutional and impact investment.

Its system includes a 50-watt solar panel with a lithium-ion battery. It uses digital payment services to allow for the payments, with the basic service costing only $6 to set up and then $6 a month thereafter. Upgrades are available after just a few months of payment. Of the 1.3 billion people who reportedly have no access to electricity in the area, $30 billion apparently is spent on kerosene. This kind of model will significantly impact that.

AKON LIGHTING UP AFRICA

Akon Lighting Africa has a very interesting background: founded by R&B and Hip Hop Star Akon, rated the Most Influential African Musician by Forbes. The solar power initiative has grown tremendously quickly, spanning 15 African countries since starting up in just 2014. "Our initial aim was to impact a million homes, but now we're in 15 east-African countries. Not having electricity growing up and then going to the U.S. where I got used to having clean water and light and visiting my family in Africa only to see that not much has changed within a span of 20 years or so is really what inspired me to begin this initiative," Akon said at the Re-energising the Future Renewable Energy Track in 2015.[107]

With a million dollar credit line with banking partners, Akon Lighting Up Africa has been able to enter each of its operating countries and speak directly to governments, working out their needs, their budget, and then coming up with a plan quickly due to their pre-financing. The company is also quite vigorous in creating training programmes and several other projects — including joining Shell in its #makethefuture smart energy programme.

Lagos in Nigeria was the site of Shell's first African solar- and human-powered football pitch, after having also established one in Rio de Janeiro. The #makethefuture campaign is about "putting bright ideas" into communities. A football pitch was refurbished with more than 90 underground tiles that actually capture kinetic energy from the players on the pitch, and transform that energy into lighting for the pitch itself, helped by solar power. This kind of power is experimental, but it's thought that it would work well in cities.

CREATING ELECTRICITY FROM GRAVITY — A FASCINATING VIDEO FROM THE #MAKETHEFUTURE CAMPAIGN.

Akon truly believes the continent has all it needs to create renew-

---

107   See AfriZap, *According To Akon, Renewables Will Dramatically Disrupt Africa's Energy Sector. Here's why.* Accessed at www.afrizap.com/en/akon-africa.

able, sustainable energy. "New, reliable and smarter energy solutions play a major role in driving human progress in Africa," he says. "Projects like this innovative football pitch draw attention to the major opportunity that Nigeria, as well as the whole of Africa, have if we look to better harness new technologies and the continent's abundant renewable energy resources."

The pitch was also featured in a music video. This kind of collaborative effort really makes younger people think out of the box and get excited about their continent and nation.

This kind of thinking of using human-powered energy is a very interesting concept. Billionaire Manoj Bhargava has been looking to harness the idea, inventing a bike that generates electricity as you pedal, and then that electricity helps to power up a small home. One hour of exercise on a bike can power a home for up to 24 hours. Since transport with bikes is a popular form of getting around in Africa, the solution is a very interesting one. While this idea hasn't come from Africa, but rather from India, it's interesting to see how much innovation is happening around this simple, basic idea.

GIGAWATT GLOBAL

We now turn our eyes from solar power in the home to solar power grid technology. 2015 was the year that Rwanda finished its 8.5MW solar power plant, built in the shape of Africa with 28,360 solar panels, sitting in neat rows amidst Rwanda's verdant, rolling hills. As you enter it you need to go under a sign that says, "Arise, shine for your light has come," - a play on a Biblical verse.

What's interesting about it is not only the scale, but also how quickly it was built. From the contract being signed (at a cost of $23.7 million) to it being connected to the grid, it took just a year. In the process it created 350 jobs and has now increased Rwanda's generation capacity by six percent (about 15,000 homes). Rwanda wants to see half its population powered up and connected by 2017.

The panels don't sit stationary but track the sun throughout the day, which improves efficiency by 20 percent. It was built by Gigawatt Global, Norfund and Scatec Solar, which is backed by Barack Obama's Power Africa initiative. The field can be monitored easily via the Internet. Many of those involved in the project believe it's a sign of the future.

There are other spin-offs, not just the power generated. Villagers nearby, especially the youth, often receive training. It has also created much interest in solar power itself amongst locals, with one girl inventing solar panels of her own.

FAR TO GO, BUT GETTING THERE

All this innovation excites me. We have far to go in connecting Africa's energy, but it's so fantastic when you see what is actually happening on the ground. Who knows? Africa might lead the way in clean energy after all.

"Our children may learn about the heroes of the past. Our task is to make ourselves the architects of the future."

- Jomo Kenyatta, the First President of Kenya

CHAPTER TWELVE

DRIVEN TO INNOVATE: TRANSPORT

C reating and maintaining suitable transport infrastructure continues to be one of the continent's greatest challenges. Success in this area will bring huge rewards, allowing for freedom of movement for people and companies, and the ability to unlock many of the continent's mineral wealth deposits. Infrastructure with roads, rail, bridges, harbours, airports is all needed for an efficient transport system. With an increasing growth in urban environments, transport solutions are becoming more complex.

In many ways, technology hasn't progressed in any major way when it comes to transport. No one has invented a flying car that's practical, or a teleportation device that works right off an app on your smart phone! So when I thought of this chapter, finding transport solutions that will create major change was difficult.

Nevertheless, there have been a few disruptive startups and fun ideas. For example, Bamboo Bike.

BAMBOO BIKE

Bicycles are cheaper than cars or motorbikes, of course, but for many in Africa they can still be too expensive. But there is a way of circumventing the cost, drastically. That is, to make the bike out of bamboo - which is everywhere. It's highly sustainable from an environmental point of view, but bamboo is also very flexible, making it an ideal material for bicycle manufacture.

Making a bicycle out of bamboo isn't new or novel — it's been around for a hundred years, in fact. But it's picked up in popularity quite recently after Craig Calfee, a renowned bicycle designer, launched Bamboosero in 1995 in California, U.S.A. — which focuses on making stylish bamboo bikes, particularly in developing countries. Since then many African companies have begun to manufacture these bikes, with many different models - from road to city to mountain bikes, male and female versions. The bicycles are also bespoke, adding to the stylish-ness of it all.

One organisation is riding this trend in Ghana: Boomers International. Not only are its bamboo bikes an effective transport solution, but they are increasing youth employment at the same time. Its primary goals is to alleviate poverty. Some of its apprentices have even been trained by Calfee himself.

Kwabeno Danso, founder and CEO, says he wants to conquer the world with bamboo in the next five years. He is looking at branching out into furniture, household items, and even houses made of the stuff. It's an example of how Africa can be at the forefront of interesting, more environmental solutions.

EASY TAXI

We now get to the more disruptive businesses, such as Easy Taxi, which links very much into digital payment services.

Easy Taxi is much like Uber, and it's not some new competition but has been around for quite some time. The app allows for you to basically set up an account, call a cab, and pay for it all through the app. In Africa, cashless transactions are truly a win, because of the many safety challenges, for one. But Easy Taxi's linking into M-Pesa and other digital payment services makes it a brilliant contender on the African landscape. This allows for Easy Taxi to provide a service for people without smart phones and access to the app, but with older mobile phone technology. All the users have to do is go to their M-Pesa menu, enter in the business number (176207), the driver's unique driver code, and how much the fare was. After the user types in their PIN the payment goes through, and they receive a receipt which they can show to the driver.

This kind of seamless and accessible system opens up the ability for more people to use transport of this kind. Users with smart phones can also pay through the app, all cashless - either by credit or debit cards, or M-Pesa. In fact, M-Pesa transactions can go straight to the driver's M-Pesa account.

Interestingly, Easy Taxi has also launched a service linked to Microsoft Outlook, where an email will remind the user of an event or meeting in their calendar, and giving the user the ability to request a taxi right there.

Easy Taxi has become Kenya's fastest growing taxi hailing app, and it has its sights set on other countries as well, especially with how well its partnership with M-Pesa is working.

SNAPSCAN

In a similar vein is the app SnapScan, a Standard Bank initiative, which looks to solve parking problems, especially in urban contexts.

In many malls and parking lots, you have to keep cash on you to pay for parking. Often the parking machine can be quite a pain. It could ask you to pay R8 for parking in South Africa, for example, and refuse to take any notes above R50. If you only have a R100 note, you've got to somehow find change — either ask someone or hope a shop attendant would be willing to help you (they generally aren't, given the amount of people that come in on a daily basis and ask!). You can try and draw cash from an ATM, but the ATM might insist you can't draw less than R100, and you're not guaranteed that you're going to get the cash as one R100 note or five R20 notes.

SnapScan seeks to avoid this inconvenience, and increase safety in the process, by allowing you to pay for your parking through the app on your smartphone. It also works in the city where parking marshals are given special ID cards that have a SnapScan QR code and a parking agent number.

The solution is really simple. Scan the QR code on the parking ticket or the parking marshal's ID card in the SnapScan app, enter your Standard Bank account PIN, enter the amount to pay, and after the debit goes through, in a matter of seconds, your parking ticket will automatically be registered as 'paid'. All you do is present it at the exit and away you go. Or, in the case of a parking marshal, they receive an SMS telling them that the parking is paid for and you receive a printed parking receipt.

CHECK OUT HOW SNAPSCAN WORKS IN THIS VIDEO.

SnapScan also let's you pay for goods and services through your phone, and has actually been working in the restaurant business for several years. You can even buy Big Issue magazines at intersections with it. South Africa has seen a big uptake, with 14,000 businesses signing on at the time of writing. It's one way in which African cities are becoming truly technologically driven, and one way that at least some of the transport challenges are being overcome.

INSPIRATION
Innovation in transport has a long way to go, but I think that the more people are inspired by what's out there, the more people will begin to uncover new, brilliant solutions. Africa has unique challenges and it can provide unique solutions that may cause a revolution.

"Whether you're a farmer, builder or engineer, the opportunities are equal: Just add a little innovation."
— **Strive Masiyiwa, Zimbabwean Businessman, Entrepreneur, and Philanthropist.**

CHAPTER THIRTEEN

AGRICULTURE AND THE FUTURE

Innovations in agriculture in Sub-Saharan Africa is a vast topic, and there's a lot that can be said around new seed and fertiliser technologies, policy changes, scientific research, crop performance, genetics, and so on. I won't go into all that as it's not my field. I will, however, focus on how mobile applications have changed people's lives on the ground.

INSURANCE

I covered the amazing benefits microinsurance brings to agriculture in chapter 8. I mention that here so that you know why I'm not going to go into detail again. But it's worth reiterating that by providing a viable, affordable insurance solution to farmers, families and whole communities reap the benefits. One natural disaster can ruin a farmer's livelihood for ever, and they will simply never be able to recover, sending their whole family into a poverty cycle. Microinsurance has allowed for such things to be circumvented — all through finding a way to deliver the insurance by teaming up with digital payment services and telecommunications.

They key point made in the microinsurance space is that finding solutions for African people in their context and culture is absolutely imperative. Corporations need to look at the *actual* needs of the people and come to meet them. They need to look at the *actual* culture and meet it where it's at. The reason why I mention this is because I'm going to re-iterate this highly important point by looking at three apps that do precisely this: iCow, M-Farm and Livestock Wealth.

ICOW

ICow is simply an app for small-scale dairy farmers in Kenya. It's SMS and voice-based, so the farmers don't even need a smartphone. It's essentially a mobile phone cow calendar. What's that, you ask? Well, to put it more succinctly, it's a "virtual veterinary midwife" - which is how Forbes likes to put it. It helps farmers track the estrous cycle of their cows, giving them tips for cow breeding, nutrition, gestation, milk production efficiency, and more. Farmers receive SMS messages on the vital days of their cows' gestation period, and they are also given details of the nearest vet.

All farmers have to do is register by sending a message to iCow's phone number. They're then asked a series of questions about their cows - like weight and calving dates. The app works out all the cycles and so forth from this information and then begins to help the farmer along.

By helping farmers with their cows, it upskills them and increases their financial returns. The cow mortality rate is greatly reduced by just knowing the right information. These farmers don't have access to the Internet to go looking, especially since answers won't necessarily even be in their language. So this is a particularly African problem addressed in an African way.

M-FARM

M-Farm is another Kenyan innovation for farmers. Much like iCow, the app provides information to farmers, but this time in the form of market prices.

Farmers are typically not able to keep in touch with the market, and usually they have to rely on the information given to them from those people who are buying from them. That opens the door wide-open for unfair practice. Pricing transparency is key in any fair deal, and M-Farm helps to ensure this happens. It also links farmers directly to buyers, taking away the opportunity for a middle man to take advantage.

Via the app or via SMS, farmers receive daily messages about the market on 42 crops sold in five markets. In an interview with Wired.co.uk,[108] Jamila Abass, the 29-year old computer scientist who invented the app, talks about how unfair things can get for farmers:

> "Many farmers only have the produce, but don't have the means to market their produce themselves. They have to rely on middlemen who show up and give them both the price and the buyer. They have no information and no alternative market. We wanted to close that information gap between the farmers and the market," says Abass.

But Abass quickly realised the negative outcome of farmers having this kind of information: they could lose the only buyers

---

108   See Wired, *MFarm empowers Kenya's farmers with price transparency and market access.* Accessed at http://www.wired.co.uk/news/archive/2013-06/21/mfarm

they have. Buyers aren't spoiled for choice. The other interesting development is that certain enterprising individuals have come to the market to create a trading platform that many of the farmers have simply not been ready for. Scepticism on the market is quite high given how even non-profit organisations have not fulfilled their obligations.

The root cause of most of the unfairness, according to Abass, was not actually access to pricing information but the actual amount of produce the farmers are able to provide. The urban markets want to buy from one supplier, not several, which is why middlemen got involved in the first place. To counteract this problem, the app itself acts as a kind-of middleman — one with the farmers' interest in mind. Through the app, farmers can 'team up' with each other to sell particular produce at certain drop-off points. They send an SMS to the M-Farm system explaining what it is they are selling. This information immediately becomes available to buyers.

The group tool also works with buying, allowing farmers to team up and buy their supplies, such as fertilizer, together. By teaming up they have access to bulk pricing, or the ability to put their resources together to buy what they all need.

M-farm manages the transactions through mobile money, including M-Pesa, of course. But the money can also go straight into bank accounts. Buyers place orders through the app and these orders are communicated to farmers, who then go to the designated drop-off points with their product. They SMS the system to let buyers know they are there. Buyers collect the goods and verify both the quality and quantity through M-Farm. M-Farm releases the money to the farmer once everything is confirmed as okay. M-Farm even takes care of even, or selected, distribution amongst farmers when it's a group sale.

M-Farm takes a transaction fee from every transaction using the platform. (It also makes money by selling research which the app collects.) Studies have now shown that farmers can effectively double their sales by simply using this app. It lowers the cost of supplies, puts them in touch with better pricing and margins, and also a consistent market. Plus it provides information on what is going on in the agricultural scene, so that farmers are not surprised. For example, if a certain pesticide is banned, farmers (who are not on the platform) might not know, and only discover when a buyer arrives and rejects their goods. M-Farm, however, can keep the farmer informed.

The app is now looking at the export market and believes it can provide a social upliftment scheme through this. Could such an app begin to affect markets worldwide? You know, I think it just might. An interesting, innovative mobile solution, that is truly changing people's lives, fuelled by the water in the innovative space: digital payment services.

LIVESTOCK WEALTH

Owning cattle is a sign of wealth in Africa, and it is often used in negotiating *lobola* (a dowry, for my Western readers). Many younger people cannot truly afford to have ten or twenty cows, and besides, living in an urban area makes this impossible.

But what if there was a way where you could own a cow without having to actually house the cow? And take care of it? And have land for it to graze on?

Enter Livestock Wealth, where urbanites can own cattle. Through the app, users can put money into a traditional African "asset class" (in other words, cattle) as an investment. Buy a cow for R10,500 and pay Livestock Wealth R295 a month to take care of it. Another R99 gets you insurance for the cow. The cow's offspring is sold to abattoirs and you get a dividend from that sale. Once the cow reaches eight years old, you get a replacement at no extra cost. You can even go and visit your cow, or see it through a 'virtual kraal'.

Ntuthuko Shezi, from South Africa, believes the app can actually turn all the cattle found in small, inefficient herds across the country, into actual annuity income, while freeing up the land for crop farming. There are, on record, 13 million head of cattle in South Africa and half of that are part of small herds in rural areas that belong to otherwise poor people. Keeping the cows there, where the grazing is bad and the water is scarce, is actually not making good use of them. Rather, they can serve better somewhere else.

According to the stats, 75 percent of South Africans don't understand what shares and unit trusts and bonds are about. But they do understand cows. That's why the slogan of the company is, "shares are difficult, cows are easy" and "We exist to change the way Africa invests".

The emotional connection Africans share with cows is something that Livestock Wealth understands. People don't have an emotional connection with shares, but having cattle brings a sense of pride. The idea is to deliver returns to investors of 8 to 12 percent, depending on the price of beef. The collective sale of the calves to the abattoirs is split equally between cow owners. Everyone shares profits and losses. When the cow gets too old it gets sold to the abattoir, and that money is what is used to replace it with a new one at no cost to the investor.

In the long run, the company intends to launch a cow-exchange programme, where beef cows are exchanged for milk cows. The small, rural farmer will receive milk cows for their beef cows, the former which are more practical for the rural farmer as they can provide produce and an income opportunity.

It's the kind of thinking that truly shows how Africa is approaching its culture and finding ways to create income in its own context and setting. I wonder to myself - could such a scheme be applied to insurance? What if, by signing up with a particular service provider, you get a digital payment service where you can buy a cow? That kind of investment would make a lot of sense to many Africans. When you see the amount of ways in which all these innovations can link up, the Africa of tomorrow can be a very exciting, creative, and technological space.

"As Africans, we need to share common recognition that all of us stand to lose if we fail to transform our continent."

- Thabo Mbeki, Former President of South Africa.

CHAPTER FOURTEEN

THE AFRICAN FUTURE

As we've uncovered throughout this book, Africa has a bright future, and innovation has the potential to truly open long-shut doors on the continent. I've had the tremendous pleasure of featuring some amazingly impressive innovation (and innovators) on my radio slot. Many are clearly resonating with my audience, while others still have a road to travel before consumers understand what they're doing.

BIG CHANGES

A partnership with Facebook and Eutelsat to bring full satellite coverage to all of Sub-Saharan Africa, with West, East and Southern Africa, is due to launch in late-2016. It's an example of something big simmering under the surface that many people don't really understand, but will bring a big change. Having Michel de Rosen, CEO of Eutelsat on the show gave me an opportunity to dig a bit more into the partnership and its roll-out plans. I'm highlighting this here because it truly shows how Africa is changing. This is, in my personal opinion, one of the biggest game changers to come, as it completely side steps the need for traditional infrastructure that the mobile operators currently provide, in one swoop! With instant internet coverage to all of Sub-Saharan Africa and with the rate at which quality of VoIP-type calls (Skype, Whatsapp, etc.) are improving, having a mobile contract may soon be a thing of the past. As a Eutelsat press release says, "Using state of the art satellite technology, Eutelsat and Facebook will each deploy Internet services designed to relieve pent-up demand for connectivity from the many users in Africa beyond range of fixed and mobile terrestrial networks. Satellite networks are well suited to economically connecting people in low to medium density population areas and the high throughput satellite architecture of AMOS-6 is expected to contribute to additional gains in cost efficiency." Mobile operators beware! This may be pushing things too far with the possibilities but that's exactly what happens when entrepreneurs start to think outside the box.

INNOVATIVE TRENDS TO CONSIDER

Having featured quite a number of innovations out of Africa on the radio show, with more to come, some aspects have started to become quite apparent. I've been fascinated by these recurring trends I've being seeing in these features. The three that have clearly stood out have been:

1. **Innovation that excites is very simple.** And it's simplicity that always speaks to a specific need in the community. Note the SMS theme across the innovations we've discussed in this book. Most consumers are already accustomed to SMS as a communication tool. Piggy backing off this means that adoption of technology is high and the need for customer education is low.

Another theme is Unstructured Supplementary Service Data (USSD) which is almost always available regardless of airtime or data availability, and can be accessed on any phone — a feature or smartphone. You get access to millions of Africans instantly without them having to do more than they already do.

2.   There is an untapped eco-system. It hit me like a ton of bricks when I realised putting all these innovation systems together would create an ecosystem that the world hasn't seen and may probably not be prepared for. Just think about it. Put the innovations I've talked earlier into a practical context. Grandma Nojongile ("Gogo"), who was blind and used the Vula App to detect her cataracts, will need to call family, friends and health practitioners on her way to the hospital for her surgery. The more calls she makes the more free health cover she gets using MicroEnsure's free insurance cover on the back of airtime spend. When she gets to the doctor for her operation, she's covered. The doctor prescribes medication which she buys on the way home, but confirms is genuine via SMS, using Sproxil's technology. She gets home, turns on her pay-as-you-go Mkopa Solar product and voilà, she's got electricity.

Far-fetched? I don't think so. These innovations are spread all over Africa without knowing the other exists. There is a big opportunity for an entrepreneur to harness this. Now wouldn't that be interesting?

3.   It costs the consumer almost nothing. I did some high level calculations and the above eco-system would only cost Gogo about 40 US cents a day, above and beyond her current daily spend.

• Being checked by the health practitioner using the Vula App — Free.

- Getting health insurance from MicroEnsure — Free.
- Confirming her medication is genuine using Sproxil — Free.
- Turning on the lights when she gets home using Mkopa — 40 US cents based on her usage.

There is so much that can happen in this space. Technology is developing at a tremendous pace, and much of it (if not all) can contribute to innovation changing the way we view Africa and also in opening up new services and industries. This book has been my attempt to unpack, uncover, and - hopefully, even - unleash this technology to many of us who aren't expecting it, but will find it improves our lives.

But there are two more trends that I've seen the longer I've been in this space. Both of them I include here to encourage us in Africa to think differently, which we are so clearly capable of doing.

1. WHERE WE CAN IMPROVE: EQUALITY

I was sitting in a meeting with one of the top print and digital media companies in South Africa, where we were discussing running an innovation segment in print. It was a very positive meeting and once again it dawned on me that innovation is one of the ways we are going to change the African story.

As we were finalising the strategy for the implementation, one of the ladies said to me, "So, when will you be able to send us a list of female entrepreneurs you've featured?" Until that point I hadn't even thought of the innovation features on the radio show in terms of gender, but it was glaringly obvious that I hadn't featured any females on the show! I had to do some quick thinking in the meeting as to why and I realised it wasn't for lack of trying, but there just weren't many female entrepreneurs in the innovation scene. I did eventually manage to find a few, and it has helped to set a precedent which I now actively try to encourage.

We need more African female entrepreneurs. One of my hopes is that this book, and this sentence, will encourage more female entrepreneurs in the scene to step up. I would love to feature more of you on the show, so please contact me so I can do so! My contact details are at the end of this book.

2. WHERE WE CAN IMPROVE: AFRICAN FUNDING

Where are the African Venture Capital (VC) funds? On the radio show, I have also managed to showcase successes of some of the innovations we've previously featured. More often than not, the success of these innovations is defined by a funding partner investing in these businesses. But I don't actually see enough African VC funds investing in these startups.

This can mean only one of two things — either VC funds don't believe in our African innovation, or they don't know about these innovations. I hope to be part of the solution as I can contribute to the latter. Either way I believe it's our prerogative as Africans to not only tell our own story, but to fund our own stories. Clearly international investors see something in our innovation. It'll be a very sad if we woke up in five years' time and realised we had no control of our innovations. Africa VC funding — it's time to rise!

Sometimes, I think, this is also a matter of how success stories are portrayed in the media - how we write and speak about these stories. In general, it's big news when an overseas investor puts money in. The question is: why? I've no doubt many journalists and those involved in media will read this book, and if that's you, my encouragement is we should think of how we can report on this differently. How we speak and write about successful startups and entrepreneurs needs to change. I'm probably even guilty of this in portions of my book and it might take some time for this ship to change direction.

OUR NEW AFRICAN NARRATIVE

I hope you've enjoyed this book and feel as fired up about Africa as I have been in writing it. This is a continent full of creativity and potential. We have an exciting future in Africa and technology is driving a great deal of it. But more than technology, African thinking is driving it. Change is coming, and we must get on board. Who knows what the world will look like if the financial inclusion and innovation vision finally becomes a reality? After decades, even centuries, of looking for solutions to so many of the world's problems, I think we're on the cusp of a new revolution. It's in our hands, today. In all of our hands. And it's coming from Africa.

Africa is rising!

ACKNOWLEDGEMENTS

My parents, Mr & Mrs. Oranye — for sacrificing everything, literally to make sure I have the best education money can buy, even if it was out of their financial means. I'm truly blessed and grateful to have parents like you.

My lovely wife, Nkhesani who always told and reminded me that I have a lot to contribute to the world and, moreso, Africa.

My siblings — for always looking up to me and being proud of my achievements. Love that never dies.

Victor Kgomoeswana — for believing that I had something to contribute on his show and letting me host the Innovation Segment every Thursday on PowerHour, PowerFM 98.7. I'm eternally grateful for the intro into the radio world. The show inspired me to write this book.

My many friends and colleagues who religiously listened to me on the radio show every Thursday and wanted podcasts when they missed it. Your encouragement is deeply, deeply appreciated.

I dedicate this book to all the African entrepreneurs and professionals who aren't afraid to see the potential of our beloved Africa and, more impressively, doing something to actively change our narrative. I humbly salute you.

ABOUT NNAMDI ORANYE

Nnamdi Oranye, dubbed "The Innovation Guru" on Power FM 98.7's weekly innovation segment with Victor Kgomoeswana, is passionate about the power of technology and innovation to change the lives of Africans. His many travels and business experience across the continent have greatly contributed to his huge optimism for Africa and its bright future. He features frequently as a presenter and chairperson across various conferences in Africa, contributes regularly to media houses on the subject of innovation, and has been named amongst the 100 most influential names in Africa's telecoms, media and ICT industry by the AfricaCom100 Research Board.

CHECK OUT NNAMDI'S ONLINE PROFILE BY SCANNING THIS QR CODE.

Please enjoy the following three chapters from Nnamdi's book,
Taking on Silicon Valley:
How African Innovators Will Shape Its Future

Today's Africa is an amazing place full of change and creativity, and its tech innovators are at the forefront of its transformation. That's why Silicon Valley has woken up to Africa's massive potential and clearly has its eyes set on the continent. And not only is Silicon Valley interested, but China as well.

But what will it mean when the tech "big boys" of Silicon Valley and China, who have repeatedly disrupted industries all over the world, set up shop in Africa? Will this bring positive or negative change? And how can African innovators not only compete with the world's tech giants but even take them on?

These are the questions Nnamdi Oranye seeks to answer in his thought-provoking book, "Taking on Silicon Valley," a follow-up to his previous book, "Disrupting Africa: The Rise and Rise of African Innovation." Africa has an amazing future, and it is its innovators who will shape it. There is a way Africa can take on Silicon Valley. It requires for eyes to be opened to the past, the present, and the future; for dreams to be taken seriously; and for African innovators to keep steady on the path they are so passion-ately forging.

Taking on Silicon Valley is available wherever good books are sold.

TAKING ON
SILICON VALLEY

HOW AFRICA'S INNOVATORS WILL SHAPE ITS FUTURE

"In today's world, paradoxically, it is the boldest action that is often the safest. Remaining where you are in a world that is changing so rapidly is in fact the most dangerous of all places to be in."

— **Hakeem Belo-Osagie**

CHAPTER ONE

×

SILICON VALLEY RISES

1939, Palo Alto, California, U.S.A.

A garage.

It's the tail-end of the Great Depression, with international affairs going awry and war looming. T.V.'s are not common household items, and people in the newspaper are still identified by their home addresses. If you had to glance at the classified section in the local newspaper you would find ads for "the removal of dead livestock," "Winchester Hi Quality Chicks: hatching every Thursday", or even "an analysis of whether your soil is sweet or sour." Phone numbers are still only four digits.

Palo Alto is a beautiful little town, which got its name from a tall coast redwood tree named El Palo Alto, which can still be seen there today. Palo means 'tree' in Spanish and alto means 'tall'. So hence, 'tall tree'. It was originally established by a railroad tycoon, Leland Stanford Sr. in 1885, when he also founded Stanford University—in honour of his son, Leland Stanford Jr, who died tragically of typhoid fever at the age of 15.

Stanford wasn't an instant success in the same way it is today, and spent many years in financial struggle after its founder died. Things went from bad to worse in the massive 1906 San Francisco earthquake, which did significant damage to Stanford, and devastated eighty percent of San Francisco — it had the highest death toll of any natural disaster in California's history. Stanford rebuilt, but it would only be many years later that this university would become a world-renown leader in innovation and technology.

Professor Frederick Terman is the man who really started it all, who had the vision. One might even want to consider him to be Stanford's second founder. He would be known as a very serious and detailed man who was passionate about what he wanted to accomplish, dressing in suits and wearing old-fashioned shoes and always driving a second-hand car. Two bright students of his, David Packard and William Hewlett, are thinking of starting an electronics business, but they don't really know how to get started.

"I did a number of little things then to help get their business started," Terman told Stanford in 1985. "A new idea in electronics (the so-called 'resistance-tuned oscillator') turned up. I told Bill, 'It looks to me as if you could use this to make an instrument. It would be a lot simpler and cheaper than anything on the market. But you'll have to solve a couple of problems to make it function.' Bill came up with an absolutely perfect solution. He designed and built an audio oscillator, a device that generates signals of varying frequencies. To remove serious instability, Hewlett took advantage of the nonlinear resistance-temperature characteristic of a small light bulb. The addition of one standard and inexpensive component turned a balky laboratory curiosity into a reliable, marketable instrument.[1]"

This is the kind of thing Terman would do. He wouldn't just have his students innovate and dream and come up with new things, but he would discover ways in which what they invented could actually be marketed and used in existing industries. Packard, in 1939, had already graduated and was working for General Electric. But he gave that up for a lower salary, moved back to Palo Alto, and rented the lower floor of a duplex with his wife. Behind the house was a small garage. This would be the garage that would later inspire millions of entrepreneurs and geeks for decades, even up to today, and be dubbed "the Birthplace of Silicon Valley." Today, it's a historical landmark, and you can go see it. They needed to call their new-found company something, so they thought they would just use their names. But they couldn't decide whose name should appear first. Therefore, they turned to a coin, flipped it, and it favoured Hewlett. Their company was therefore called Hewlett-Packard. No doubt you've heard of them.

They received an initial investment of $538 (about $9,263 in 2016) and Terman managed to raise further money for them to help them with a salary. Their first product was a device for bowling alleys that would indicate automatically if the bowl was a foul. It was very clever, but no one really saw any value in it, and so was ultimately a market failure. They then decided to turn to the oscillator, which Terman also saw value in. So they invented an audio frequency oscillator which caught the attention of Walt Disney Studios, who wanted to use it for the soundtrack for its upcoming movie featuring Mickey Mouse, Fantasia. World War II, surprisingly, was great for the business too. They initially

---

1   *Fred Terman, the Father of Silicon Valley.* By Carolyn E. Tajnai. Available at http://forum. stanford.edu/carolyn/terman

marketed through mail orders and, during the second world war, grew their company significantly by building radar, nautical, aviation, radio and sonar devices. Hewlett-Packard, or HP as it is known today, eventually became the world's biggest producer of measurement and electronic devices — a major producer of calculators, personal computers, laptops, printers, and other items. It was not just the technological innovation that led to the company's great success, but also the innovative ways in which Hewlett and Packard ran it. "What I'm most proud of is the fact that we really create a way to work with employees, let them share in the profits, and still keep control of it," Hewlett would frequently say.[2]

HP was the first of many, many more examples to come. The area soon became a thriving hub of innovation. But Terman and his team had an even bigger vision — to build an industrial park and tie the emerging industries, existing industries, and university together. This took the area during the 50's from an innovative hub to a thriving centre of startup businesses, forming what many first called the Valley of Heart's Delight and became known as Silicon Valley in the 70's. More than two thousand electronics and information technology companies exist there today. Terman would always call it their 'secret weapon'. "When we set out to create a community of technical scholars in Silicon Valley, there wasn't much here and the rest of the world looked awfully big," he said once. "Now a lot of the rest of the world is here.[3]" He is right. And today, Silicon Valley is in the rest of the world — in your pocket or on your desk or at your bedside right now, probably.

But what does all this have to do with Africa, you might ask?

---

2   *William Hewlett & David Packard: Maverick Managers.* Published at Entrepreneur Magazine, October 2008. Available at https://www.entrepreneur.com/article/197644

3   *Fred Terman, the Father of Silicon Valley.* By Carolyn E. Tajnai. Available at http://forum.stanford.edu/carolyn/terman

The answer, as far as I'm concerned, is everything. What I've highlighted above is the standard, stock story. But there is more to it. It's worth probing exactly *why* Terman encouraged these two men to do what they did, what opportunities came their way, how they took hold of these, and what was all bubbling under the surface at the time. I mean, it was the Great Depression and war was on its way, arguably the kind of time when risk-taking is not highly encouraged. Terman himself would tell stories of how they had literally nothing to work with. "An accident that burned out a few vacuum tubes or damaged a meter would produce a crisis in the laboratory budget for a month," he once said. "The pre-war electronics laboratory was in an attic under the eaves, over the electrical machinery laboratory. The roof of the attic leaked, and at times these leaks became quite bad. There was no money to repair the roofs, so they built big wooden trays and lined them with tar paper and tar. As the trays filled, we walked around them. Our morale didn't suffer. One winter Bill Hewlett added a homey touch by stocking the trays with goldfish.[4]" Terman and his colleagues were working upstream, against what was arguably a prevalent culture of safety, not risk. Yet they forged ahead and took a risk with a brand new sort of business and with emerging technology that was quite frankly unprecedented.

Over the years it only got better. Stanford produced advancement in research and saw dozens, then hundreds of companies, and now thousands form through what it was doing. It set the culture and pace for what has made Silicon Valley so highly innovative and productive, to the point that today the term "Silicon Valley" no longer just refers to the place but has become a synonym for anything hi-tech, innovative, enterprising, and disruptive. Thousands of inventions, Nobel prizes, strong academia,

---

4   Ibid

and an entrepreneurial spirit now characterise Stanford and the Silicon Valley it has effectively built.

It seems to me Frederick Terman *saw* something of the future. Risks were opportunities. And he encouraged his bright minds to see it that way. Where we are right now in Africa, we need to somehow see what he saw, but *for us*. Obviously, our context is different, but we have to start somewhere, just like they did at the end of the 30's. We have to experiment, innovate, test, and play. Timothy J. Sturgeon, writing in the book by Kenney Martin on how Silicon Valley came to be, highlights that "perhaps the strongest thread that runs through the Valley's past and present is the drive to 'play' with novel technology, which, when bolstered by an advanced engineering degree and channelled by astute management, has done much to create the industrial powerhouse we see in the Valley today." We need to have this kind of thinking — there is a real sense in which we, in Africa, need to take assimilate some of this philosophy. Did all of that happen by accident? Of course not. Did that sort of thinking emerge on its own? Of course not. Under Terman's leadership, Stanford embarked on building "steeples of excellence" — networks of science and engineering researchers, a "community of technical scholars," who would entice the brightest and best students to the university. Terman fostered close relationships with students and technologies and industries emerging at the time. He encouraged his students to form companies of their own and personally invested in them, with money and time and emotional input. Today some of those students, in addition to Hewlett and Packard, include the founders of Litton Industries (a large defense contractor) and Varian Associates (a high-tech company specialising in electromagnetic equipment). After the war, as dean of the School of Engineering, he got the University to lease portions of its land to hi-tech firms, encouraging companies such as General Electric (and the aforementioned companies) to move in to the Stanford Industrial Park, which is the bulk of Silicon Valley. What he did, essentially, is he brought like-minded, like-hearted people *together*. He believed in them, invested in them, and saw that the future was theirs.

In an article, his son Lewis Terman highlights three core elements of his father's strategy. "There is the government money, there's the university, and the industry. He wanted a tight tie together between industry and the university with the government money supporting education of the students who would then go into the industry. That was the model he was working on that he thought had really great opportunities to do great things." Terman's vision was undoubtedly to create a true technological hub that involved human elements like community, study, and a pioneering spirit.

Of course, it's the Internet that has really made Silicon Valley a prominent player on the world stage today. But that would never have come about without the foundations that were set. Google started at Stanford when founders Larry Page and Sergey Brin developed their algorithm in the 90's. (Yahoo also emerged from Stanford, from alumni Jerry Yang and David Filo). At the time of writing this book, Silicon Valley is just two decades from turning a hundred years old. It has firmly entrenched itself not only into American culture, but into the culture of the world, and it continues to do so in overt and subtle ways. Today its presence is felt when you wake up, go to sleep, and walk around — all there in your pocket in that little device called your smartphone. And the idea of that itself comes from a philosophy, not just an idea but a way of *thinking*, that developed within Silicon Valley.

Sometime in the 80's its core philosophy became the 'personal'.

It started with the personal computer. Adverts from Microsoft in the 80's can be found on the Internet, with Bill Gates quotes as saying, "A computer on every desk, and in every home, running Microsoft software." This was a new idea in those days — especially the idea of bringing the computer into the home. "I think it's fair to say that personal computers have become the most empowering tool we've ever created," Gates would say in the following years. "They're tools of communication, they're tools of creativity, and they can be shaped by their user." These days, the smartphone is the new version of that — and in fact, it seems Steve Jobs took Bill Gates' vision and realised it needed to go beyond a computer on a desk, but a computer in your pocket. All of this innovation, of course, means that today Silicon Valley holds a huge and prominent position in how economics, politics, and business is discussed and executed, even if it's not yet clear exactly what it will all mean. Its influence on our world is unprecedented. Its influence on Africa is felt in ways we probably would never have imagined, especially when it comes to the mobile phone and the incredibly huge way that simple invention is allowing us to leapfrog traditional infrastructure. Africa's mobile penetration is growing exponentially, and everyone knows that if we can solve the Internet connectivity issue, Africa will present the biggest market in the world next to China.

There is a 'dark side' to all this, however. Silicon Valley is not just about innovation and business and technology but is also starting to become a synonymous term for negative elements like "big business", corporate takeover, hostile takeovers, monopolising industries, and a new kind of technological colonialism. In Silicon Valley's own era of Facebook and Google and Amazon, it's easy to see why some people have started becoming almost afraid of the way things are developing, especially when we look at how much of our own world is run by these giants, and when we see how these companies are cannibalising so much of what's happening out there. Further to this, it gets even darker, with WikiLeaks recently releasing details of CIA code that showed just a little bit of the extent of its hacking capabilities and efforts — from hacking smart TV's and gaming devices and phones and listening in on your conversations; being able to read your messages before they're encrypted; and even taking control of smart cars to drive into a wall and assassinate an enemy. Technology has, indeed, become both the blessing and the curse the sci-fi writers always envisaged it would, and as we explore what some of Silicon Valley's brightest innovators are doing, you will find what those sci-fi writers dreamed is actually not far off.

Recently, I touched down at Jomo Kenyatta airport in Nairobi and instantly connected to Wi-Fi at the airport. I remember the days when you would first head off to a stationary shop to buy a map, would need to perhaps find a telephone to call the taxi company; or to call the company you've come to see and ask them where their lift was, and you would perhaps call the hotel you booked to confirm your booking. You'd have to find their number somewhere in a folder with a stack of other paperwork, and you would head next to the foreign exchange to cash in your traveller's cheques. What a slow world that was — although we would complain about how fast-paced life was!

Once on Wi-Fi, however, I first opened up Google maps to confirm the location of the hotel and its distance. I used Google Maps' travel feature to give me an idea on the location of my hotel. Satisfied with what I saw, I opened the app and called an Uber (yes, 'uber' has become a noun). Of course, I didn't need to worry about drawing any money — Uber is linked to my credit card, and my credit card works internationally anyway, so paying for my hotel won't be an issue as well. Google Maps helped me just to get a bearing of where my meetings would be, and I went through a few emails to confirm my itinerary.

The phone beeps. "Your Uber ride is 2 minutes away." Great, I've got my bags, I'm off to the exit. "Your Uber ride is 1 minute away." I track my ride's every movement through the app. I get out the exit and stand on the sidewalk for a few seconds, looking for the car that matches the description on the app. Ah, there it is. "Your Uber ride is here!" Great, I get in, greet the driver, confirm his name, and sit in the back feeling relaxed. There are a ton of innovators I'm off to meet, and I start to think about how each of them can create a difference on our continent. Lately, I've been thinking a lot about how our innovators can take on Silicon Valley—how we would be able to create our own technology giants here that could compete or partner with Silicon Valley in ways that are beneficial to us. I think of some of the industries Silicon Valley has disrupted on our very continent, and I think of what we need to do to ensure it all works for our benefit.

I freeze. Something in the back of my mind just sparked. My conscience, perhaps, or a sudden realisation. I look at my phone, I see the Uber ride moving on the map, showing me how far I am from my destination.

"I just did it!" I blurt out loud. "It was me!"

My Uber driver looks at me in his rearview mirror.

"Um. Sorry. Excuse me, sir?"

"Uh," I reply, frowning. "Um. Never mind."

I realise what it is I just did. In the space of five minutes, I have just disrupted several massive African industries. I was part of the disruption. I was the one who opened these apps and used them and loaded my credit card in them. I was the one who ultimately sent this revenue to Uber in California. Uber drivers themselves in Kenya aren't paid very much — and there have been several issues with how it is slashing prices in the third world, making drivers get paid even less. How would this all have worked if Uber wasn't here, I wonder?

I worry about the taxi guy who's probably out of a job because I ordered an Uber. What about his family? What will he do now? I think of how I'm creating demand for this service and being such a typical consumer. I think about the touristy conversations I may have had with a taxi driver because I used to take note of the landmarks and my surroundings, so I could get to grips with how to get around town. Now I don't even think about that anymore, as I know I can just rely on my phone and my maps there and whatever the Uber app tells me. I think about the printers and the cartographers involved in making maps in the old days. The entire process which I've just circumvented with my phone. That makes me think about the tourism industry. What about the tourist guides? The myriad of people who would connect you with a strange, new city?

Is what I've done a good thing? A bad thing? What do we do? And why didn't I rather try and find an African alternative to use? I look at my phone in my hands and I think about the telecommunications companies in South Africa where I've just come from. I think about the thousands of jobs that might be affected because I don't use international roaming capabilities anymore. I just use my data and Wi-Fi wherever I go—WhatsApp calls, messaging, email, everything I need. All giving California an advantage.

My mind won't stop ticking as I analyse the pros and cons of disruption. I think of Henry Ford and his T-Model cars and how it disrupted the horse and carriage industry — relegating it to a sporting activity we maybe now watch at the Olympics, if perhaps we're bored. I wonder if some our prominent industries would become relegated to "sporting activities". I think about which one of these could be. I rationalise that at a macro level, disruption is good for our growth as a continent, and I start a mental checklist of the positives and negatives. I remember articles I've read, ones that I've written, conversations I've had, the innovators I'm about to see, and then I'm covered by a deep sense of responsibility.

Because I realise I need to do something. It would be a travesty if our kids and the next generation only learn about Silicon Valley disruptors. I can see it now: lessons at school on Mark Zuckerberg, Larry Page, Brian Chesky, Travis Kalanick and …? What? No African innovators?

There has to be an "and". This is critical. There just has to be an "and". We need to be learning about these disruptors and our disruptors. It cannot be any other way. This book is about helping our innovators become that "and".

"There has to be an 'and'", I say out loud.

My Uber driver looks at me in his rearview mirror again.

"Excuse me?" he says.

"Oh, uh, never mind. Again." I reply.

"Er. So, er, where you from?" he asks.

In a way, I'm grateful for the interruption. It gives me some space to come down to earth, to engage with the real people involved. In between our chit-chat, I know that this book has to be written and has to be distributed across Africa. Because Silicon Valley has its eyes on us. The Big Boys of Google, Facebook, Uber, Amazon, and others are all looking for fresh opportunity on fresh cyber-soil, and we're in the target zone. They're here already, and they're here to stay. There are many positive to these winds of change blowing through our continent, and many of them are working to create positive change, such as better connectivity and the likes. But there are also many negatives as whole industries are upended. More than anything I believe we need to be ready for this because if we are not we are going to run into some serious trouble — and I was only just briefly skimming the surface of it in my wandering, worrying thoughts at the back of an Uber.

"Without change there is no innovation, creativity, or incentive for improvement. Those who initiate change will have a better opportunity to manage the change that is inevitable."

— **William Pollard**

THE TIPPING POINT

A t a TEDx talk in London in 2014, Tanzanian Billionaire and founder of the Infotech Investment Group, Ali Mufuruki, came out with a guns-blazing statement: "Africa is not rising."

"I think that there is quite a number of profound flaws to the Africa rising narrative. The first one being, we are coined not by an African, but a well-meaning Western journalist. Somebody who's standing outside, looking in. And comparing the state of the continent today to what it was fifteen years ago. Obviously, it's better today than what it was fifteen years ago. And we have embraced that narrative without questioning it, and I think that's why we are where we are."

I remember watching this and thinking to myself that Mufuruki might be gunning down the wrong enemy. In my own work in the field, I've found he is in line with what many others are saying. These days, there are many journalists and media representatives who look a bit sheepish when we speak of "Africa Rising". I've been told its old news, that it's just been a dream, and if I want to be relevant today I better find a different narrative or some other way to spin things It's become almost popular to disparage this much-beloved narrative.

I finally got the opportunity to meet Mufuruki on a panel at a conference in Durban, South Africa. I finally got to understand what he meant. Mufuruki's reasons for saying what he said at TEDx was that we need to be realistic. From there, he went on to highlight several industries and challenges where he says there has not only been stagnation but regression. They were mostly the usual suspects — electricity, technology, education, amongst others. We all know this, and I don't think we should keep quiet about it. But there's far more than this going on. I've found the more time I spend there, the more my optimism increases. My optimism is based on realism — on what I actually see and experience happening with African people and entrepreneurs. I've taken a look at all these usual suspects and I've spent a great deal of time investigating what's going on with our innovators, and in my book, *Disrupting Africa*, I highlighted how innovation is morphing each of them and allowing us to dream up new technologies that leapfrog traditional infrastructure. I still believe that. Since starting my journey of cataloguing innovations, it's only gotten better. And this is why we must foster our innovators.

My parents' generation came out of the colonial era. Most of them either experienced the tail end of colonialism or the start of independence and revolution. In my own experience, I've found the common theme with most of my parents' generation was that you must get a good education. Most of them fought for that and some of them were able to actually experience what education is like or were able to make it into a professional career. Education was something you aspired to, a sure sign of success. Whether you were in Nigeria, South Africa or Kenya, the trend was the same. There was also a tie-in to the type of leadership my parents' generation had as well. Most of the leaders that came out of that era really promoted education and professionalism and epitomised it themselves. Think of Kwame Nkrumah, Nnamdi Azikiwe of Nigeria, Nelson Mandela, and even Robert Mugabe. These were professionally educated leaders that inspired the educated spirit and showcased that education is the key to strong, rational, independent leadership.

But there is more to this story. If you fast forward twenty to thirty years later, to where we are today, it's not far off (even if it's controversial) to say the leadership of that time effectively failed the education cycle. I've just found that too many of those from that generation have all of a sudden found they have no pension. What do they do now? And this is not just an African thing — this is one of the reasons why there is so much political turmoil in the world, as the system from previous years has failed a generation, and a new generation does not want to find themselves in a similar position.

I believe that one of the factors that has led to this is around how we viewed leadership, and therefore how we viewed entrepreneurship. It was a big deal for me to think of entrepreneurship as an actual career choice, as I related in the previous chapter. Being an 'entrepreneur' in Africa about thirty years ago meant that you sold tomatoes or oranges on the side of the road because you were unable to get a job anywhere else due to a lack of education. Obviously, this meant you didn't have the brightest future and governments should do something about it. You never aspired to be an entrepreneur, you aspired to get a good education and get a good job.

The next generation after my parents, which I belong to, obviously, have realised that this set up has not really worked. We still view education as important, of course. I certainly do. I think it's critical. For many, the set up has worked, but it hasn't delivered on all its promises. I can't see myself working for the next thirty years and finding out I have no pension, and I'm sure you're much the same. Moreso, education hasn't always meant you are able to get a job in Africa and contribute to Africa. In fact, it's often meant the exact opposite. Which has created a real problem for us with the diaspora, who have often found they need to come back to the continent but yet there is no work.

This problem, however, has created an interesting situation that we can (and ought) to take advantage of. According to Ndubuisi Ekekwe, founder of the non-profit African Institution of Technology, the Great Recession brought many African intellectuals with unique skill sets back home, because job opportunities ran out overseas. However, faced with the reality that job opportunities for their skill set in Africa were a dime a dozen, they began to use their skills to create markets, find solutions, form companies, and be entrepreneurs.

"The collapse of the commodity boom has pushed countries and their citizens to invent other ways to survive because benefits like unbridled imports are no longer sustainable. Now many things are coming together which will help transform some African economies by the sheer power of their entrepreneurs. The cloud, open source software, cheap computing resources, and ideas from local technology hubs are redesigning Africa. Even if the commodity boom returns, these structures will remain because they are homegrown and well-designed. In fact, it shows promise for a golden era of entrepreneurship anchored by local innovation.[5]"

This is exciting. It shows the positive side of why Mufuruki and many others are going negative on the African Rising narrative, saying we need to have a "reality check" in light of the downturn in China's economy which marked an end to the commodity price super-cycle that was driving a great deal of the economic growth of our continent. In a Sunday Times opinion piece, Jabulani Sikhakhane continues in the same mood: "Narratives about sub-Saharan Africa's economic growth have swung, during the past four decades, between two extremes: pessimism and exuberance. After much exuberance about Africa's strong growth over the past two decades, albeit driven by a few countries, the tide is turning back to despair."

However, the positive effect of this is we see African intellectuals with specific skill sets returning to our continent and being forced to take up entrepreneurship and innovate. This is why my work in researching, cataloguing, and writing about innovation, as well as connecting innovators together, has made me think differently to the two extremes Sikhakhane highlights above. I agree emphatically that Africa Rising isn't going to happen just because we talk about it or think positively about our continent. I understand the general sentiment. We want to be realistic. It's okay to dream, but we need to also just face the facts. But I believe we can justify the narrative and go beyond just talking about it, but to actually quantifying it today (and not to some distant future) by looking at our innovation. We need to look at the right things in the right places and in the right way. We need to be putting on the right set of spectacles to really see what's going on.

---

5   *Why African Entrepreneurship is Booming*, by Ndubuisi Ekekwe. Published at Harvard Business Review, July 2016. Available at https://hbr.org/2016/07/why-african-entrepreneurship-is-booming

The system of 'study and get a job' has shown itself to be unsustainable for the long run, and arguably the Great Recession itself showed this to be the case. Many people living in what we call "developed nations" have felt this problem themselves, and many find themselves out of work because they are actually overqualified. There is such a thing as too much education, or rather, a purposeless education. You have to be educated to be going somewhere, not just to have a degree. What is the solution for overqualified people? Probably entrepreneurship. The trouble is, in the Western world, not only are they without employment, they have a massive student loan to service as well! Which makes taking a risk with entrepreneurship even more difficult to do, even perhaps out of reach. In our context, however, it might be different—and many of those who are innovating in the education space here in Africa have seen this and have been working at creating a new solution for us. There is a new wave of entrepreneurs coming out of the woodwork and looking at opportunities, grasping them, and exploding into success. Some of these I will highlight later in this book because how they think is important to think about. And this has certainly created a change of culture. We grew up with our parents instilling in us that you have to be a professional, and we never looked at entrepreneurs as the rock stars like they are today. We always equated entrepreneurship to someone struggling to get by or that they have not really done well in school. But now that's all flipped 180 degrees. Entrepreneurship has come to be seen as a pathway to success and a test for true leadership. Sure, we have to be careful with how we romanticise it. This isn't an easy path to take, I can assure you. But I want to encourage you to not be like me and only think of it as a viable alternative when you're well into your working career. Hopefully, you're in your mid-twenties and younger. That's not to say that you can't make the dive when you're older, only that you have a lot more risks to take.

We have gotten to a stage from an innovation point of view where we understand the basics, but we need a clear roadmap from here to fifty years from now to see what our legacy will look like. As opposed to just focusing on the challenges we have had or the opportunities we did not have, we must appreciate where we have come from and what we have done really well. One of the ways in which we need to do this, I believe, is to challenge the 'developing world' narrative head-on, and thus take our Africa Rising narrative seriously. We have to challenge present-day thinking around concepts such as "development" and a "developed nation". To apply Mufuruki's thoughts about Africa Rising to these terms, I say that we have "embraced" this "narrative" about how a nation should develop "without questioning it." And "that's why we are where we are." To be frank, I think he's right about some of our mistakes, but we now need to aim at the right target.

AFRICAN INNOVATION IS AFRICAN

With that, let's look at all this from a different angle. In mid-2016, I read an opinion article at CNBC by David Levin, entitled *Why Africa is missing among the Worlds Top Innovators*. The article seemed to be loosely based on the Bloomberg Innovation Index's "Fifty Most Innovative Economies" in the world. As the author rightly points out, Africa hardly featured on the list at the time. "How can this possibly be?" Levin asks. He continues:

> "How can there be no contribution from sub-Saharan Africa which contains two of the three largest economies on the continent as measured by GDP? From the stand-point of innovation — and by extension — contribution to

the greater global good, Africa wasn't even on the map (pardon the pun). Of course, theories abound with respect to what plagues Africa — and there are plenty to choose from. I know what you're thinking. Poverty, corruption, electricity, food security, African strongmen, water, sanitation, land, terrorism, etc. And you're all correct. Unfortunately, these rationalisations all contribute to the distasteful reality that Africa is an emerging market that has, well... never quite emerged. It's stuck in the mud.[6]"

Levin shares my frustration and trumpets the opinion that the best way through is via education. I agree, although in some circles this answer has become a bit of a cliché, and I've already highlighted the limits of education above. The issue then, as far as I'm concerned, isn't whether or not education is the missing key but rather *how* we do education that matters. The history of Silicon Valley is a case in point. Education really happens when we put people and ideas together and create a community, which creates an ecosystem. Teaching goes far beyond academics but involves the full experience and exposure to industry and smart people. This goes beyond innovation hubs and the like.

I must admit Levin's article bothered me quite a bit, and for more than just his comments on education. I spent a few days trying to figure it out and then it hit me. I had just published my book filled with credible African innovators and could fill up another book based on new innovators I was coming across, and realised that Bloomberg's assessment is simply incorrect. When you look at what's happening on the ground, to deduce that Africans (beyond Morocco and Tunisia) do not innovate, you find a very different story emerging. The lack of visibility of

6   *Why Africa is Missing Among the World's Top Innovators*, by David S. Levin. Published at CNBC Africa, July 2016. Available at http://www.cnbcafrica.com/news/2016/07/07/why-africa-is-missing-among-the-worlds-top-innovators/

African innovators and their inventions does not mean they do not exist. But there were other problems I had with the general sentiment of the article. I argue that Africa faintly featuring on the global map of innovation has less to do with whether Africans are innovating and more to do with the faulty preconceptions about the people of the continent and, quite frankly, a poor understanding of what innovation and its purpose actually is. Have you actually ever tried finding a definition for innovation? You get very vague answers. Google's dictionary simply says it is "the action or process of innovating." It further qualifies this by saying it refers to "a new method, idea, product, etc." That doesn't really say much. So how do we measure something as vague as innovation? The reason why innovation is difficult to define is because it requires *context* — it requires an antithesis of sorts, or a problem, an opposite.

Finally, my disgruntlement was also a culmination of being irked by another narrative of African countries classified as "developing". This idea paints the picture of a continent that is slowly tracking its way from a "developing" to a "developed" status. Perhaps it strikes you as odd that I would take issue with this, but follow my train of thought for a bit. The definition of a developed country (according to Wikipedia) is "a sovereign state that has a highly developed economy and advanced technological infrastructure relative to other less industrialised nations". The word "industrialised" jumps out quite vividly for me. For most people, I imagine it invokes imagery of factories, production and manufacturing on a large scale. Fair enough. This is important and I don't discount it. However, what is implied is that the future of African countries — the path we must travel — is defined by the past of other nations. It presupposes that in order to trans-form, Africa must copy and paste the trajectory that other continents undertook. This view of development insinuates that there is only one way to a bright future, one way to progress, and that to transition from "developing" to "developed", Africa must follow this path and emulate the industrialisation trends of other continents that have been fortunate enough to be classified as "emerged".

I beg to differ. Allow me to add a little more to the thought process here before I show why. Let's turn our attention to the Bloomberg Innovation Index, as I mentioned above, which takes a similar tack. Every year it attempts to measure the top 50 most innovative countries in the world. In 2016 it scored South Korea at the top, with the U.S. coming in at eighth. Only two African countries made the list, both in the bottom ten. In 2017, South Korea still came tops, with Sweden climbing to second and Finland making it into the top five. Russia went down fourteen spots to No. 26, while the U.S. jumped down one spot further to ninth place. China still held its title as the strongest ranked emerging market. According to Bloomberg in 2016, this makes South Korea 'the leader in the world of ideas'. I know they are amazing, but does this mean that they come up with all the good ideas? If that's the case, why have they not solved so many of the problems we face as the world? I answer: *because they aren't looking to solve our problems, but theirs.* Perhaps Magnus Henrekson, quoted in a Bloomberg article discussing the 2017 index, scratches on the surface when he says, "In the [Nordic] culture, people are super individualistic — this means that people have ideas and are very interested in pursuing them in this way in order to become wealthy. The incentives are there and the tax system favours them.["][7] In other

---

7   *These are the World's Most Innovative Economies*, by Michelle Jamrisko and Wei Lu. Published at Bloomberg Markets, January 2017. Available at https://www.bloomberg.com/news/articles/2017-01-17/sweden-gains-south-korea-reigns-as-world-s-most-innovative-economies

words: their focus is for themselves, and I don't think that's a bad thing, it's just that we need to be aware of it.

Let me go further. What definition does Bloomberg use for innovation? How is it working this out? Firstly, it defines innovation as "the creation of products and services that make life better".[8] This is also very vague as it is, and it implies that the actual environment — in other words, what's happening on a grassroots level, is not taken much into account. So I went to look at the methodology. Bloomberg looks at how much money is invested in research and development, manufacturing and patent activity, and other metrics. These are all very difficult to measure across borders, because patent laws, for example, are different everywhere. The bottom line, however, is that when one looks at the details an interesting pattern emerges: *the ideology of industrialisation still drives the metrics by which success in development is measured.* I realise that we obviously aren't going to find a perfect system to measure everything, and I submit the Bloomberg Innovation Index is incredibly helpful (and challenging). But I still am led to ask an obvious question: is it *really* innovation if it's measured by the old story of *industrialisation* and if this is measured by those who have already gone through that story?

Perhaps it also strikes you as strange to hear me say that industrialisation is the old story. I realise I'm simplifying things a bit to try and make a point. I also realise I'm going against the grain in a big way. But after connecting with African innovators, entrepreneurs and paradigm-shifters from across the continent over the past four years, it's clear to me that Africans

---

8   See Three Views (and Methodologies) on Global Innovation, by Kevin Stahler and Jan Zilinsky. Published by Peterson Institute for International Economics and available at https://piie.com/blogs/north-korea-witness-transformation/three-views-and-methodologies-global-innovation. This article provides a great overview of the challenges faced by these sorts of innovation indexes, and the different methodologies involved.

want a new story, not an old one. We're living in the 21st century, which calls for a new path to development. The old story is not going to cut it in this world's future, and Silicon Valley knows that, so why don't we?

I am not saying we ought to throw out everything and start again, rejecting the industrialisation narrative because we want to arrogantly claim some sort of self-identity independent of everyone else. In fact, I'm saying the exact opposite. We are where we are, but what are we going to do about it? We need to take what we learn from others and use wisdom to apply what we learn to our continent, rather than try and just copy in some form or another. We cannot, to quote Mufuruki again (but use his statements differently) accept the industrialisation narrative "without questioning it." It seems odd to me that the Africa Rising narrative is held up to such scrutiny while we give the industrialisation narrative a free pass. Perhaps you say it's because it's already shown to work. I say, sure, it's worked there, but it's not working *here*—because we have different challenges to face. Perhaps you say it's because we have had all these problems in the past: colonisation, oppression, Apartheid, etc. I'm saying that *yes we have*. And note, *they didn't*. They had other issues to face, and these were not the same as ours. And even so, many instances of their success was done on the back of Africa and our people, and we are not going to make our success on the back of some other nation or people. So, therefore, we cannot expect to just emulate and see things work. The industrial revolution and subsequent development didn't happen in a vacuum, it happened in an entire context and history and pre-industrialised period which set the groundwork and foundation for it to work from.

This is all why Africa needs to be defined by what is uniquely African. And I firmly believe we can see the Africa Rising narrative becoming a reality when we look at African innovation. Nobody understands African challenges the way Africans do— they experience them every day. They are best placed to find innovative solutions to their problems, and they do. Innovation is about changing people's lives in *their* world. It should not be limited by what people in a different context think is valuable.

HERE ARE A FEW EXAMPLES TO ILLUSTRATE

In 2016, Dr Valentin Agon from Benin finally completed formulating his Api-Palu solution, which presents a new, cheaper, and more effective way to test for malaria, using a simple plant extract. Dr Eddy Agbo, from Nigeria, is also an African innovator taking on the same challenge. He invented a new 25-minute test for malaria that costs approximately $2.

Until now, the only way to test for the disease has been through blood samples, the results of which can take days to receive. According to the World Health Organisation (WHO), there were 214 million cases of malaria in 2015 worldwide. It goes without saying then that these two innovations are revolutionary for the continent. These change lives. But if both these innovators allowed themselves to be defined by the so-called 'tried and tested' methods, which work in other contexts but aren't working in ours, how many lives would they save?

Malaria is one of Africa's biggest challenges. Two Africans have found innovative solutions. When we look at the innovations coming out of the 2016 Innovation Prize for Africa (IPA), we cannot help but be positive. But it is interesting, and disheartening, to note that these kinds of innovations do not fit the definition of what the Bloomberg Innovation Index and other references define as innovative.

Ntuthuko Shezi, a South African innovator, is another example of an African approach to finding solutions to African problems. His app, Livestock Wealth, is a uniquely African innovation in the investment space. The majority of South Africans may not understand what shares, unit trusts and bonds are, for various reasons. But they do understand cows, which in many African cultures are considered an investment. Shezi's starting point for his innovation was a simple question: what if there was a way to own a cow and have it taken care of without having to house it? The concept appeals to many African urbanites. And that's what Livestock Wealth does — through the app, users can put money into a traditional African "asset class" (in other words, cattle) as an investment. One buys a cow for about R10,500 (about $800) and pays Livestock Wealth R295 (about $23) a month to take care of it. Another R99 (about $8) buys insurance for the cow. The cow's offspring is sold to abattoirs and the owner gets a dividend from that sale. Once the cow turns eight years old, a replacement can be acquired at no extra cost. The owner can even visit the cow, or see it through a 'virtual kraal'.

I can understand why someone in the U.K. or North America or Japan may not relate to this sort of innovation, but that doesn't mean that it isn't innovative. It is solving a local problem for local people. Sure, innovations like Uber or Airbnb are changing entire industries, and they are disrupting Africa, too—we will devote considerable time to unpacking that in this book. However, much more is happening on the ground, where it matters, than too many people realise.

Ugandan-born Ashish J. Thakkar — CEO of the Mara Group, a highly successful global conglomerate, once heard a young African girl say, "Don't blend in — blend out." In other words, be a unique individual. This wisdom, I believe, is for the Africa continent as a whole. No longer do Africans want to blend in with the old story.

On the contrary, we want to blend *out*, to forge a new way, and to innovate according to our realities. Thakkar is a fascinating case study in this direction. Like him, I ask in my own way: is there some sort of natural law that means development and progress can only follow one path? Of course not. Through collective creativity, Africans can find a unique path. The old ways of thinking are simply proving not to work for us, who have a different context and a different history to deal with. We must use them where appropriate, adjust as needed, but also pioneer something of our own. I've seen this happen. If we put our innovations together, something exciting emerges: a new eco-system that creates a very exciting future that can leapfrog tradition infrastructure.

To illustrate my point when I speak to people regarding this, I ask the question, "What would be considered more innovative for Africa: A high-speed train into rural locations in Africa or a solar grid that kicks in when the national grid is offline?" Almost everyone says the latter because that's the most innovative solution for Africans. Then I proceed to tell them that this already exists in Rwanda. Their eyes always light up!

Yes, Africa is rising, and on its own terms. Perhaps redefining development is just what it needs. African innovation is tangibly changing lives, even without garnering the visibility it deserves, because it does not seem to fit into the pre-determined, acceptable metrics for what development and innovation are. I have no doubt that consistency, creativity and support will get us there.

I also have no doubt that if we do not innovate, Silicon Valley will do it for us. And so, now we turn to seeing just how Silicon Valley is coming to us, and how we need to approach this technological invasion to make it fit in with Africa Rising.

"Without change there is no innovation, creativity, or incentive for improvement. Those who initiate change will have a better opportunity to manage the change that is inevitable."

— **William Pollard**

×

CHAPTER THREE

IS THE AFRICA RISING NARRATIVE DEAD?

At a TEDx talk in London in 2014, Tanzanian Billionaire and founder of the Infotech Investment Group, Ali Mufuruki, came out with a guns-blazing statement: "Africa is not rising."

"I think that there is quite a number of profound flaws to the Africa rising narrative. The first one being, we are coined not by an African, but a well-meaning Western journalist. Somebody who's standing outside, looking in. And comparing the state of the continent today to what it was fifteen years ago. Obviously, it's better today than what it was fifteen years ago. And we have embraced that narrative without questioning it, and I think that's why we are where we are."

I remember watching this and thinking to myself that Mufuruki might be gunning down the wrong enemy. In my own work in the field, I've found he is in line with what many others are saying. These days, there are many journalists and media representatives who look a bit sheepish when we speak of "Africa Rising". I've been told its old news, that it's just been a dream, and if I want to be relevant today I better find a different narrative or some other way to spin things It's become almost popular to disparage this much-beloved narrative.

I finally got the opportunity to meet Mufuruki on a panel at a conference in Durban, South Africa. I finally got to understand what he meant. Mufuruki's reasons for saying what he said at TEDx was that we need to be realistic. From there, he went on to highlight several industries and challenges where he says there has not only been stagnation but regression. They were mostly the usual suspects — electricity, technology, education, amongst others. We all know this, and I don't think we should keep quiet about it. But there's far more than this going on. I've found the more time I spend there, the more my optimism increases. My optimism is based on realism — on what I actually see and experience happening with African people and entrepreneurs. I've taken a look at all these usual suspects and I've spent a great deal of time investigating what's going on with our innovators, and in my book, *Disrupting Africa*, I highlighted how innovation is morphing each of them and allowing us to dream up new technologies that leapfrog traditional infrastructure. I still believe that. Since starting my journey of cataloguing innovations, it's only gotten better. And this is why we must foster our innovators.

My parents' generation came out of the colonial era. Most of them either experienced the tail end of colonialism or the start of independence and revolution. In my own experience, I've found the common theme with most of my parents' generation was that you must get a good education. Most of them fought for that and some of them were able to actually experience what education is like or were able to make it into a professional career. Education was something you aspired to, a sure sign of success. Whether you were in Nigeria, South Africa or Kenya, the trend was the same. There was also a tie-in to the type of leadership my parents' generation had as well. Most of the leaders that came out of that era really promoted education and professionalism and epitomised it themselves. Think of Kwame Nkrumah, Nnamdi Azikiwe of Nigeria, Nelson Mandela, and even Robert Mugabe. These were professionally educated leaders that inspired the educated spirit and showcased that education is the key to strong, rational, independent leadership.

But there is more to this story. If you fast forward twenty to thirty years later, to where we are today, it's not far off (even if it's controversial) to say the leadership of that time effectively failed the education cycle. I've just found that too many of those from that generation have all of a sudden found they have no pension. What do they do now? And this is not just an African thing — this is one of the reasons why there is so much political turmoil in the world, as the system from previous years has failed a generation, and a new generation does not want to find themselves in a similar position.

I believe that one of the factors that has led to this is around how we viewed leadership, and therefore how we viewed entrepreneurship. It was a big deal for me to think of entrepreneurship as an actual career choice, as I related in the previous chapter. Being an 'entrepreneur' in Africa about thirty years ago meant that you sold tomatoes or oranges on the side of the road because you were unable to get a job anywhere else due to a lack of education. Obviously, this meant you didn't have the brightest future and governments should do something about it. You never aspired to be an entrepreneur, you aspired to get a good education and get a good job.

The next generation after my parents, which I belong to, obviously, have realised that this set up has not really worked. We still view education as important, of course. I certainly do. I think it's critical. For many, the set up has worked, but it hasn't delivered on all its promises. I can't see myself working for the next thirty years and finding out I have no pension, and I'm sure you're much the same. Moreso, education hasn't always meant you are able to get a job in Africa and contribute to Africa. In fact, it's often meant the exact opposite. Which has created a real problem for us with the diaspora, who have often found they need to come back to the continent but yet there is no work.

This problem, however, has created an interesting situation that we can (and ought) to take advantage of. According to Ndubuisi Ekekwe, founder of the non-profit African Institution of Technology, the Great Recession brought many African intellectuals with unique skill sets back home, because job opportunities ran out overseas. However, faced with the reality that job opportunities for their skill set in Africa were a dime a dozen, they began to use their skills to create markets, find solutions, form companies, and be entrepreneurs.

> "The collapse of the commodity boom has pushed countries and their citizens to invent other ways to survive because benefits like unbridled imports are no longer sustainable. Now many things are coming together which will help transform some African economies by the sheer power of their entrepreneurs. The cloud, open source software, cheap computing resources, and ideas from local technology hubs are redesigning Africa. Even if the commodity boom returns, these structures will remain because they are homegrown

and well-designed. In fact, it shows promise for a golden era of entrepreneurship anchored by local innovation.[9]"

This is exciting. It shows the positive side of why Mufuruki and many others are going negative on the African Rising narrative, saying we need to have a "reality check" in light of the downturn in China's economy which marked an end to the commodity price super-cycle that was driving a great deal of the economic growth of our continent. In a Sunday Times opinion piece, Jabulani Sikhakhane continues in the same mood: "Narratives about sub-Saharan Africa's economic growth have swung, during the past four decades, between two extremes: pessimism and exuberance. After much exuberance about Africa's strong growth over the past two decades, albeit driven by a few countries, the tide is turning back to despair."

However, the positive effect of this is we see African intellectuals with specific skill sets returning to our continent and being forced to take up entrepreneurship and innovate. This is why my work in researching, cataloguing, and writing about innovation, as well as connecting innovators together, has made me think differently to the two extremes Sikhakhane highlights above. I agree emphatically that Africa Rising isn't going to happen just because we talk about it or think positively about our continent. I understand the general sentiment. We want to be realistic. It's okay to dream, but we need to also just face the facts. But I believe we can justify the narrative and go beyond just talking about it, but to

---

9   *Why African Entrepreneurship is Booming*, by Ndubuisi Ekekwe. Published at Harvard Business Review, July 2016. Available at https://hbr.org/2016/07/why-african-entrepreneurship-is-booming

actually quantifying it today (and not to some distant future) by looking at our innovation. We need to look at the right things in the right places and in the right way. We need to be putting on the right set of spectacles to really see what's going on.

The system of 'study and get a job' has shown itself to be unsustainable for the long run, and arguably the Great Recession itself showed this to be the case. Many people living in what we call "developed nations" have felt this problem themselves, and many find themselves out of work because they are actually overqualified. There is such a thing as too much education, or rather, a purposeless education. You have to be educated to be going somewhere, not just to have a degree. What is the solution for overqualified people? Probably entrepreneurship. The trouble is, in the Western world, not only are they without employment, they have a massive student loan to service as well! Which makes taking a risk with entrepreneurship even more difficult to do, even perhaps out of reach. In our context, however, it might be different—and many of those who are innovating in the education space here in Africa have seen this and have been working at creating a new solution for us. There is a new wave of entrepreneurs coming out of the woodwork and looking at opportunities, grasping them, and exploding into success. Some of these I will highlight later in this book because how they think is important to think about. And this has certainly created a change of culture. We grew up with our parents instilling in us that you have to be a professional, and we never looked at entrepreneurs as the rock stars like they are today. We always equated entrepreneurship to someone struggling to get by or that they have not really done well in school. But now that's all flipped 180 degrees. Entrepreneurship has come to be seen as a pathway to success and a test for true leadership. Sure, we have to be careful with how we romanticise it. This isn't an easy path to take, I can assure you. But I want to encourage you to not be like me and only think of it as a viable alternative when you're well into your working career. Hopefully, you're in your mid-twenties and younger. That's not to say that you can't make the dive when you're older, only that you have a lot more risks to take.

We have gotten to a stage from an innovation point of view where we understand the basics, but we need a clear roadmap from here to fifty years from now to see what our legacy will look like. As opposed to just focusing on the challenges we have had or the opportunities we did not have, we must appreciate where we have come from and what we have done really well. One of the ways in which we need to do this, I believe, is to challenge the 'developing world' narrative head-on, and thus take our Africa Rising narrative seriously. We have to challenge present-day thinking around concepts such as "development" and a "developed nation". To apply Mufuruki's thoughts about Africa Rising to these terms, I say that we have "embraced" this "narrative" about how a nation should develop "without questioning it." And "that's why we are where we are." To be frank, I think he's right about some of our mistakes, but we now need to aim at the right target.

AFRICAN INNOVATION IS AFRICAN

With that, let's look at all this from a different angle. In mid-2016, I read an opinion article at CNBC by David Levin, entitled *Why Africa is missing among the Worlds Top Innovators*. The article seemed to be loosely based on the Bloomberg Innovation Index's "Fifty Most Innovative Economies" in the world. As the author rightly points out, Africa hardly featured on the list at the time. "How can this possibly be?" Levin asks. He continues:

"How can there be no contribution from sub-Saharan Africa which contains two of the three largest economies on the continent as measured by GDP? From the standpoint of innovation — and by extension — contribution to the greater global good, Africa wasn't even on the map (pardon the pun). Of course, theories abound with respect to what plagues Africa — and there are plenty to choose from. I know what you're thinking. Poverty, corruption, electricity, food security, African strongmen, water, sanitation, land, terrorism, etc. And you're all correct. Unfortunately, these rationalisations all contribute to the distasteful reality that Africa is an emerging market that has, well... never quite emerged. It's stuck in the mud.[10]"

Levin shares my frustration and trumpets the opinion that the best way through is via education. I agree, although in some circles this answer has become a bit of a cliché, and I've already highlighted the limits of education above. The issue then, as far as I'm concerned, isn't whether or not education is the missing key but rather *how* we do education that matters. The history of Silicon Valley is a case in point. Education really happens when we put people and ideas together and create a community, which creates an ecosystem. Teaching goes far beyond academics but involves the full experience and exposure to industry and smart people. This goes beyond innovation hubs and the like.

I must admit Levin's article bothered me quite a bit, and for

---

10 *Why Africa is Missing Among the World's Top Innovators*, by David S. Levin. Published at CNBC Africa, July 2016. Available at http://www.cnbcafrica.com/news/2016/07/07/why-africa-is-missing-among-the-worlds-top-innovators/

more than just his comments on education. I spent a few days trying to figure it out and then it hit me. I had just published my book filled with credible African innovators and could fill up another book based on new innovators I was coming across, and realised that Bloomberg's assessment is simply incorrect. When you look at what's happening on the ground, to deduce that Africans (beyond Morocco and Tunisia) do not innovate, you find a very different story emerging. The lack of visibility of African innovators and their inventions does not mean they do not exist. But there were other problems I had with the general sentiment of the article. I argue that Africa faintly featuring on the global map of innovation has less to do with whether Africans are innovating and more to do with the faulty preconceptions about the people of the continent and, quite frankly, a poor understanding of what innovation and its purpose actually is. Have you actually ever tried finding a definition for innovation? You get very vague answers. Google's dictionary simply says it is "the action or process of innovating." It further qualifies this by saying it refers to "a new method, idea, product, etc." That doesn't really say much. So how do we measure something as vague as innovation? The reason why innovation is difficult to define is because it requires *context* — it requires an antithesis of sorts, or a problem, an opposite.

Finally, my disgruntlement was also a culmination of being irked by another narrative of African countries classified as "developing". This idea paints the picture of a continent that is slowly tracking its way from a "developing" to a "developed" status. Perhaps it strikes you as odd that I would take issue with this, but follow my train of thought for a bit. The definition of a developed country (according to Wikipedia) is "a sovereign state that has a highly developed economy and advanced technological infrastructure relative to other less industrialised nations". The word "industrialised" jumps out quite vividly for me. For most people, I imagine it invokes imagery of factories, production and manufacturing on a large scale. Fair enough. This is important and I don't discount it. However, what is implied is that the future of African countries — the path we must travel — is defined by the past of other nations. It presupposes that in order to transform, Africa must copy and paste the trajectory that other continents undertook. This view of development insinuates that there is only one way to a bright future, one way to progress, and that to transition from "developing" to "developed", Africa must follow this path and emulate the industrialisation trends of other continents that have been fortunate enough to be classified as "emerged".

I beg to differ. Allow me to add a little more to the thought process here before I show why. Let's turn our attention to the Bloomberg Innovation Index, as I mentioned above, which takes a similar tack. Every year it attempts to measure the top 50 most innovative countries in the world. In 2016 it scored South Korea at the top, with the U.S. coming in at eighth. Only two African countries made the list, both in the bottom ten. In 2017, South Korea still came tops, with Sweden climbing to second and Finland making it into the top five. Russia went down fourteen spots to No. 26, while the U.S. jumped down one spot further to ninth place. China still held its title as the strongest ranked emerging market. According to Bloomberg in 2016, this makes South Korea 'the leader in the world of ideas'. I know they are amazing, but does this mean that they come up with all the good ideas? If that's the case, why have they not solved so many of the problems we face as the world? I answer: *because they aren't looking to solve our problems, but theirs*. Perhaps

Magnus Henrekson, quoted in a Bloomberg article discussing the 2017 index, scratches on the surface when he says, "In the [Nordic] culture, people are super individualistic — this means that people have ideas and are very interested in pursuing them in this way in order to become wealthy. The incentives are there and the tax system favours them.[11]" In other words: their focus is for themselves, and I don't think that's a bad thing, it's just that we need to be aware of it.

Let me go further. What definition does Bloomberg use for innovation? How is it working this out? Firstly, it defines innovation as "the creation of products and services that make life better".[12]This is also very vague as it is, and it implies that the actual environment — in other words, what's happening on a grassroots level, is not taken much into account. So I went to look at the methodology. Bloomberg looks at how much money is invested in research and development, manufacturing and patent activity, and other metrics. These are all very difficult to measure across borders, because patent laws, for example, are different everywhere. The bottom line, however, is that when one looks at the details an interesting pattern emerges: *the ideology of industrialisation still drives the metrics by which success in development is measured.* I realise that we obviously aren't going to find a perfect system to measure everything, and I submit the

---

11   *These are the World's Most Innovative Economies*, by Michelle Jamrisko and Wei Lu. Published at Bloomberg Markets, January 2017. Available at https://www.bloomberg.com/news/articles/2017-01-17/sweden-gains-south-korea-reigns-as-world-s-most-innovative-economies

12   See Three Views (and Methodologies) on Global Innovation, by Kevin Stahler and Jan Zilinsky. Published by Peterson Institute for International Economics and available at https://piie.com/blogs/north-korea-witness-transformation/three-views-and-methodologies-global-innovation. This article provides a great overview of the challenges faced by these sorts of innovation indexes, and the different methodologies involved.

Bloomberg Innovation Index is incredibly helpful (and challenging). But I still am led to ask an obvious question: is it *really* innovation if it's measured by the old story of *industrialisation* and if this is measured by those who have already gone through that story?

Perhaps it also strikes you as strange to hear me say that industrialisation is the old story. I realise I'm simplifying things a bit to try and make a point. I also realise I'm going against the grain in a big way. But after connecting with African innovators, entrepreneurs and paradigm-shifters from across the continent over the past four years, it's clear to me that Africans want a new story, not an old one. We're living in the 21st century, which calls for a new path to development. The old story is not going to cut it in this world's future, and Silicon Valley knows that, so why don't we?

I am not saying we ought to throw out everything and start again, rejecting the industrialisation narrative because we want to arrogantly claim some sort of self-identity independent of everyone else. In fact, I'm saying the exact opposite. We are where we are, but what are we going to do about it? We need to take what we learn from others and use wisdom to apply what we learn to our continent, rather than try and just copy in some form or another. We cannot, to quote Mufuruki again (but use his statements differently) accept the industrialisation narrative "without questioning it." It seems odd to me that the Africa Rising narrative is held up to such scrutiny while we give the industrialisation narrative a free pass. Perhaps you say it's because it's already shown to work. I say, sure, it's worked there, but it's not working *here*—because we have different challenges to face. Perhaps you say it's because we have had all these problems in the past: colonisation, oppression, Apartheid, etc. I'm saying that *yes we have*. And note, *they didn't*. They had other issues to face, and these were not the same as ours. And even so, many instances of their success was done on the back of Africa and our people, and we are not going to make our success on the back of some other nation or people. So, therefore, we cannot expect to just emulate and see things work. The industrial revolution and subsequent development didn't happen in a vacuum, it happened in an entire context and history and pre-industrialised period which set the groundwork and foundation for it to work from.

This is all why Africa needs to be defined by what is uniquely African. And I firmly believe we can see the Africa Rising narrative becoming a reality when we look at African innovation. Nobody understands African challenges the way Africans do— they experience them every day. They are best placed to find innovative solutions to their problems, and they do. Innovation is about changing people's lives in *their* world. It should not be limited by what people in a different context think is valuable.

HERE ARE A FEW EXAMPLES TO ILLUSTRATE

In 2016, Dr Valentin Agon from Benin finally completed formulating his Api-Palu solution, which presents a new, cheaper, and more effective way to test for malaria, using a simple plant extract. Dr Eddy Agbo, from Nigeria, is also an African innovator taking on the same challenge. He invented a new 25-minute test for malaria that costs approximately $2.

Until now, the only way to test for the disease has been through blood samples, the results of which can take days to receive. According to the World Health Organisation (WHO), there were 214 million cases of malaria in 2015 worldwide. It goes without saying then that these two innovations are revolutionary for the continent. These change lives. But if both these innovators allowed themselves to be defined by the so-called 'tried and tested' methods, which work in other contexts but aren't working in ours, how many lives would they save?

Malaria is one of Africa's biggest challenges. Two Africans have found innovative solutions. When we look at the innovations coming out of the 2016 Innovation Prize for Africa (IPA), we cannot help but be positive. But it is interesting, and disheartening, to note that these kinds of innovations do not fit the definition of what the Bloomberg Innovation Index and other references define as innovative.

Ntuthuko Shezi, a South African innovator, is another example of an African approach to finding solutions to African problems. His app, Livestock Wealth, is a uniquely African innovation in the investment space. The majority of South Africans may not understand what shares, unit trusts and bonds are, for various reasons. But they do understand cows, which in many African cultures are considered an investment. Shezi's starting point for his innovation was a simple question: what if there was a way to own a cow and have it taken care of without having to house it? The concept appeals to many African urbanites. And that's what Livestock Wealth does — through the app, users can put money into a traditional African "asset class" (in other words, cattle) as an investment. One buys a cow for about R10,500 (about $800) and pays Livestock Wealth R295 (about $23) a month to take care of it. Another R99 (about $8) buys insurance for the cow. The cow's offspring is sold to abattoirs and the owner gets a dividend from that sale. Once the cow turns eight years old, a replacement can be acquired at no extra cost. The owner can even visit the cow, or see it through a 'virtual kraal'.

I can understand why someone in the U.K. or North America or Japan may not relate to this sort of innovation, but that doesn't mean that it isn't innovative. It is solving a local problem for local people. Sure, innovations like Uber or Airbnb are changing entire industries, and they are disrupting Africa, too—we will devote considerable time to unpacking that in this book. However, much more is happening on the ground, where it matters, than too many people realise.

Ugandan-born Ashish J. Thakkar — CEO of the Mara Group, a highly successful global conglomerate, once heard a young African girl say, "Don't blend in — blend out." In other words, be a unique individual. This wisdom, I believe, is for the Africa continent as a whole. No longer do Africans want to blend in with the old story. On the contrary, we want to blend *out*, to forge a new way, and to innovate according to our realities. Thakkar is a fascinating case study in this direction. Like him, I ask in my own way: is there some sort of natural law that means development and progress can only follow one path? Of course not. Through collective creativity, Africans can find a unique path. The old ways of thinking are simply proving not to work for us, who have a different context and a different history to deal with. We must use them where appropriate, adjust as needed, but also pioneer something of our own. I've seen this happen. If we put our innovations together, something exciting emerges: a new eco-system that creates a very exciting future that can leapfrog tradition infrastructure.

To illustrate my point when I speak to people regarding this, I ask the question, "What would be considered more innovative for Africa: A high-speed train into rural locations in Africa or a solar grid that kicks in when the national grid is offline?" Almost everyone says the latter because that's the most innovative solution for Africans. Then I proceed to tell them that this already exists in Rwanda. Their eyes always light up!

Yes, Africa is rising, and on its own terms. Perhaps redefining development is just what it needs. African innovation is tangibly changing lives, even without garnering the visibility it deserves, because it does not seem to fit into the pre-determined, acceptable metrics for what development and innovation are. I have no doubt that consistency, creativity and support will get us there.

I also have no doubt that if we do not innovate, Silicon Valley will do it for us. And so, now we turn to seeing just how Silicon Valley is coming to us, and how we need to approach this technological invasion to make it fit in with Africa Rising.

TAKING ON SILICON VALLEY: HOW AFRICA'S INNOVATORS WILL SHAPE ITS FUTURE is available online at amazon or at your local book store.
if your book store doesn't have it, ask them to order it.
ISBN 978-0620770316

T A K I N G   O N
SILICON VALLEY

HOW AFRICA'S INNOVATORS WILL SHAPE ITS FUTURE

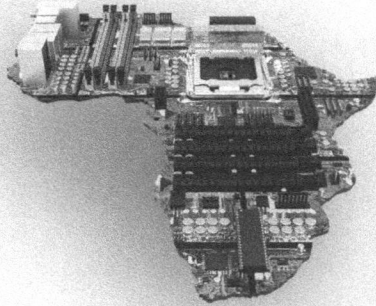

NNAMDI **ORANYE**

www.ingramcontent.com/pod-product-compliance
Lightning Source LLC
Chambersburg PA
CBHW071726200326
41519CB00021BC/6583